THE SPACE BOOK

A JOURNEY THROUGH OUR INCREDIBLE UNIVERSE

ARCTURUS

Picture Credits:

Key: b–bottom, t–top, c–center, l–left, r–right

Alamy: 30-31 (nagelestock.com), 68-69 (Photo Researchers, Inc), 92-93 (NG Images); **alexfreire:** 116br; **ESA:** 80-81 (D. Ducros),102br (C Carreau), 106cr (D Ducros); **ESO:** 38bl (Y Beletsky), 53br (Swinburne Astronomy Productions), 100br (Hubble Space Telescope), 112c (L Calçada), 121b (Y Beletsky); **EUMETSAT:** 80b; **Getty Images:** 29br (Design Pics Inc), 32-33 (Babak Tafreshi), 34tr (Oxford Science Archive/Print Collector), 40cl (DEA/G Dagli Orti), 41br (Detlev van Ravenswaay), 48-49 (Ann Ronan Pictures/Print Collector), 50-51 (Roger Ressmeyer/Corbis/VCG), 69tr (NASA/Apollo/Science Faction), 69cl (Sovfoto), 81b (Detlef van Ravenswaay), 84-85 (Stefan Morrell), 90br (Jon Brenneis); **TH Jarrett:** 87b (IPAC/SSC); **Keck Observatory:** 125cr (NRC–HIA, Christian Marois); **Max-Planck-Institut für extraterrestrische Physik:** 61b; **NASA:** 7cl (Goddard Space Flight Center/CI Lab), 10bl (JPL), 10r, 14cr, 15br (Goddard Space Flight Center/DLR/ASU), 16tr, 16cr, 17tl (JPL-Caltech/ASU), 18cl (JPL-Caltech/UCLA/MPS/DLR/IDA/Justin Cowart), 19tr (JPL/MPS/DLR/IDA/Björn Jónsson), 20cl, 22cl, 23tr, 24br (William Crochot), 27c (Robert Simmon/Chris Elvidge/NOAA/National Geophysical Data Center), 37tr, 46-47, 46b, 47tr, 54bl (NRAO/AUI/NSF/STScI/JPL-Caltech), 54c, 55bl (Caltech, UC Berkeley, Albert Einstein Institute, Perimeter Institute for Theoretical Physics, National Science Foundation/Blue Waters), 55bc (JPL-Caltech), 55br (JPL-Caltech/K Gordon, ASU), 60-61, 60br, 63cr, 63bl, 64br, 73tr (JSC), 74-75 (Bill Stafford/JSC), 74br (Mark Sowa/JSC), 75bl, 76tr, 78br, 79tr, 81r, 82-83 (JPL-Caltech), 82c (JPL/Space Science Institute), 83r (JHU APL/SwRI/Steve Gribben), 84br (JPL-Caltech/SETI Institute), 86br, 91tr (WMAP Science Team), 94c (JPL-Caltech/Las Campanas Observatory), 97tr (CXC/Stanford/I Zhuravleva et al.), 98c (Spitzer Space Telescope), 100-101 (Chandra X-ray Observatory Center), 101cr (Fermi), 103c (NASA/CXC/CfA/M Markevitch et al./STScI/Magellan/ASU/D Clowe et al., ESO WFI), 104br (JPL/ASU), 108-109 (Digitized Sky Survey, Noel Carboni), 114b, 115tr (HST/ASU/J Hester et al.), 116c (AEI/ZIB/M Koppitz & L Rezzolla), 118br (HST), 122c (ESA/S Larsen), 124b (ESA/ESO/L Ricci), 125tc (CXC/M Weiss); **Shutterstock:** 1 (Vadim Sadovski), 4-5 (Stefano Garau), 4cl (MaraQu), 4b (Viktar Malyshchyts), 4cr (NASA), 5t (tose), 5br (pixbox77), 6-7 (Vadim Sadovski), 6l (Mopic), 7t (dalmingo), 8-9 (Amanda Carden), 8bl (Jurik Peter), 8r (koya979), 9t (21), 10-11 b/g (nienora), 11 (NASA), 11b (21), 12-13 (Anton Balazh), 12l (Vlad61), 13t (21), 13b (AuntSpray), 14-15 b/g (Aphelleon), 14-15 (Quaoar), 14br (tovovan), 16-17 (Vadim Sadovski/NASA), 16b (21), 18-19 (Andrea Danti), 18b (21), 20-21 & 20cr (Vadim Sadovski/NASA), 20-21 b/g (Yuriy Kulik), 20br (Tristan3D), 21tr (21), 22-23 (manjik/NASA), 22-23 b/g (Triff/NASA), 22b (21), 23c & br (NASA), 24-25 (Vadim Sadovski/NASA), 25tr (21), 26-27 (Yuriy Mazur), 26b (vchal), 28-29 (Yiucheung), 28b (Evgenii Bobrov), 29t (Redsapphire), 30br (Designua), 32cr (Primoz Cigler), 33r (lhovik), 34-35 (SKY2015), 34bl (Vadim Sadovski/NASA), 36-37 (Oscity), 36l (I Pilon), 36br (HelenField), 38-39 (Petri jauhiainen), 38c (Wantanee Chantasilp), 39r (Muskoka Stock Photos), 40-41 (MarcelClemens), 40br (Designua), 42l (Marzolino), 43 (shooarts), 43 b/g (Stephanie Frey), 44-45 b/g (Maria Starovoytova), 44l (Marzolino), 45 (shooarts), 47br (Timothy Hodgkinson/NASA), 48l (Zbiq), 49r (iryna1), 50b (Georgios Kollidas/R Hart), 51tr (VectorPot), 51cr (BlueRingMedia), 51br (Olga Rutko), 52-53 (EastVillage Images), 54-55 (Mopic), 55c (Designua), 56-57, 57tr (NASA), 57br (bhjary), 58-59 (IrinaK), 58br (Jennifer Stone), 59tr (Zern Liew), 62-63 (Vadim Sadovski/NASA), 63tr (bhjary), 64-65 (edobric), 66-67 (3Dsculptor), 66c (Fred Mantel), 66br (stoyanh), 67tr (Georgios Kollidas), 69br (Bon Appetit), 70-71 & 70br & 71tr (Everett Historical), 71br (stoyanh), 72-73 (vicspacewalker), 73cr (Christopher Halloran), 73br (Andrew Rybalko), 76-77 (Stefan Ataman), 76-77 b/g (Viktar Malyshchyts), 76bl (Bannykh Alexey Vladimirovich), 76cr (Pavel L Photo and Video), 78-79 (Naeblys/NASA), 78bl & 79br (PavloArt Studio), 80c (Johan Swanepoel), 82bl (MawRhis), 85br (Sebastian Kaulitzski), 86-87 (MaraQu), 88-89 (chaoss), 88bl (Matt Ragen), 90-91 (Designua), 92br (vectortatu), 94-95 (NASA), 96-97 (Denis Belitsky), 96c (chainfoto24), 98-99 (NASA), 99tl (Giovanni Benintende), 100cl (Igor Zh), 104-105 (breakermaximus), 104c (Mopic), 105ct (Phongsak Meedaenphai), 106-107 (My Good Images), 109br (sciencepics), 110-111 (ESA/NASA/Herschel/Hubble/DSS), 111tl (ESO/VPHAS+ Consortium/Cambridge Astronomical Survey Unit), 111tc (Egyptian Studio/NASA), 111tr (Ken Crawford Rancho Del Sol Observatory), 112-113 (Kalabi Yau), 112br (Jurik Peter), 113tr (sciencepics), 114-115 (Jurik Peter), 116-117 (Vadim Sadovski), 117br (Catmando), 118-119 (Ken Crawford), 120-121 (Valerio Pardi), 122-123 (Tragoolchitr Jittasaiyapan), 124-125 (Giovanni Benintende); **Springel et al.:** 102-103; **Wikimedia Commons:** 24cl (Joop van Bilsen/Nationaal Archief NL Fotocollectie Anefo), 37cr (Vokrug Sveta), 49bl (Micheltb), 52c (z2amiller), 56cr (Lemuel Francis Abbott/National Portrait Gallery, UK), 59r (Arecibo Observatory), 85tl (SpaceX), 88tr, 107br (NASA/ESA/ G Bacon/STScI), 120c (Henryk Kowalewski).

ARCTURUS

This edition published in 2024 by Arcturus Publishing Limited
26/27 Bickels Yard, 151–153 Bermondsey Street,
London SE1 3HA

ISBN: 978-1-3988-3623-5
CH005077NT
Supplier 29, Date 0824, Print run 00005982

Author: Giles Sparrow
Cover artist: Lizzy Doyle
Editors: Joe Harris and Clare Hibbert
Designer: Amy McSimpson

Printed in China

CONTENTS

Introduction

Our Universe is a huge area of space made up of everything we can see in every direction. It contains a great number of different objects—from tiny specks of cosmic dust to mighty galaxy superclusters. The most interesting of these are planets, stars and nebulae, galaxies, and clusters of galaxies.

Stars

A star is a dense (tightly packed) ball of gas that shines through chemical reactions in its core (middle). Our Sun is a star. Stars range from red dwarfs much smaller and fainter than the Sun, to supergiants a hundred times larger and a million times brighter.

Planets

A planet is a large ball of rock or gas that orbits (travels around) a star. In our solar system there are eight "major" planets, several dwarf planets, and countless smaller objects. These range

Nebulae

The space between the stars is filled with mostly unseen clouds of gas and dust called nebulae. Where they collapse (fall in) and grow dense enough to form new stars, they light up from within.

Galaxies

A galaxy is a huge cloud of stars, gas, and dust, including nebulae, held together by a force called gravity. There are many different types of galaxy. This is because their shape, the nature of their stars, and the amount of gas and dust within them can vary.

This is our home galaxy, the Milky Way, seen from Earth. Our view of the Universe depends on what we can see using the best technologies that we have.

Galaxy Clusters

Gravity makes galaxies bunch together to form clusters that are millions of light-years wide. These clusters join together at the edges to form even bigger superclusters—the largest structures in the Universe.

The Sun's Family

The solar system is the region of space that surrounds our star, the Sun. It holds billions of objects, from tiny pieces of dust and icy boulders to eight major planets, some of them far larger than Earth.

Eight Planets and More

The planets of the solar system are split into two main groups. Close to the Sun there are four fairly small rocky planets. Earth is the third of these in order from the Sun, and also the largest. Farther out, past a region made up of shards and chunks of rock, there are four much larger worlds: the gas and ice giant planets.

Mars is the outermost of the rocky planets. It is just over half the size of Earth.

Venus, the second planet, is almost the same size as Earth.

The solar system formed from gas and dust left orbiting the newborn Sun about 4.5 billion years ago.

Mercury is the smallest planet and the closest to the Sun.

Earth is the only rocky planet with a large natural satellite, the Moon.

DID YOU KNOW? Astronomers measure solar system distances in **Astronomical Units** (AU). One AU is 149.6 million km (93 million miles), the same as the usual distance between the Earth and the Sun.

SOLAR SYSTEM PROFILE

Planets: Eight
Radius of orbit of most distant planet, Neptune:
4.5 billion km (2.8 billion miles)
Radius of heliosphere:
18 billion km (11.2 billion miles)
Region ruled by Sun's gravity:
Four light–years across

Where Does It End?

Astronomers haven't agreed on where exactly the solar system comes to an end. Some say it only reaches a little way past the orbits of the planets, just as far as the heliosphere—the region that the solar wind (particles streaming out from the Sun) covers. Others say it reaches as far as the Sun's gravity can hold onto objects: about halfway to the nearest star.

Jupiter is the fifth planet, and by far the largest.

Space probes have discovered changes in the solar wind as they leave the heliosphere.

Neptune, the farthest planet from the Sun, is nearly four times bigger than Earth.

Uranus is an ice giant, quite a bit smaller than Jupiter or Saturn.

Saturn was the most distant planet known in ancient times.

Saturn is famous for its rings. However, all the giant planets have ring systems—they are just a lot fainter.

7

The Sun

Our Sun is a fairly average, middle-aged star. It doesn't stand out, compared to other stars we know, but the heat, light, and streams of particles it pours out across the solar system set the conditions on Earth and all the other planets.

Solar Features

The Sun's surface is made up of extremely hot gas, with a temperature of around 5,500 °C (9,900 °F). Hot gas from inside the Sun rises to the surface, cools down by releasing light, and then sinks back toward the core. A non-stop stream of particles is also released from the surface, forming a solar wind that blows across the solar system.

Some particles are led toward Earth's poles, creating the aurorae, or northern and southern lights.

Earth's magnetic field shields it from passing solar wind.

The Solar Cycle

Some features on the Sun come and go over time. Dark areas called sunspots form and then disappear, and so do huge loops of gas, called prominences, that rise high above the Sun. Most impressive of all are outbursts called solar flares, which release huge amounts of radiation (energy) and hot gas. All this activity repeats itself every 11 years because of changes in the Sun's magnetic field.

Never look directly at the Sun—it's so bright that you risk damaging your eyes. Astronomers study it with special telescopes.

Prominences are created when gas flows along loops of magnetic field that stick out of the Sun's surface. There is usually a sunspot group at each end.

SUN PROFILE

Diameter: 1.39 million km (864,000 miles)
Distance: 149.6 million km (93 million miles)
Rotation period: Approx 25 days
Mass: 333,000 x Earth

The surface of the Sun that can be seen is called the photosphere. It marks a region where the Sun's gas becomes transparent.

Dark sunspots are much cooler than their surroundings, with temperatures of about 3,500 °C (6,300 °F).

DID YOU KNOW? Because the Sun is not a solid body, different parts of it rotate (spin around) at different rates—its **equator** spins faster than the polar regions.

Mercury and Venus

Two scorching-hot rocky planets orbit closer to the Sun than Earth. Venus is almost the same size to Earth but with a very different atmosphere. Mercury is a tiny world much like our Moon, which speeds around the Sun in just 88 days.

Roasted Surfaces

Temperatures on both Mercury and Venus reach more than 430 °C (800 °F), but Venus is actually hotter than Mercury although it is farther from the Sun. That is because Venus's atmosphere traps heat. This means that the temperature is about 460 °C (860 °F) both day and night. Mercury has no atmosphere, so temperatures on its night side can drop to -170 °C (-280 °F).

Mercury's surface has many craters (holes), like our Moon. This picture has been treated to reveal surface features.

3D view of a Venusian volcano called Maat Mons

Visiting Venus

Venus's atmosphere is 100 times thicker than Earth's, and is mostly made up of toxic carbon dioxide with sulphuric acid rain. Any human trying to land there would be choked, crushed, and cooked at the same time. Even heavily shielded robot space probes have only lasted for a few minutes. Astronomers have mapped Venus's landscape without landing there, using radar beams that pass through the clouds and bounce back from the surface to show its features.

DID YOU KNOW? Venus is the only planet whose **day** is longer than its **year**.

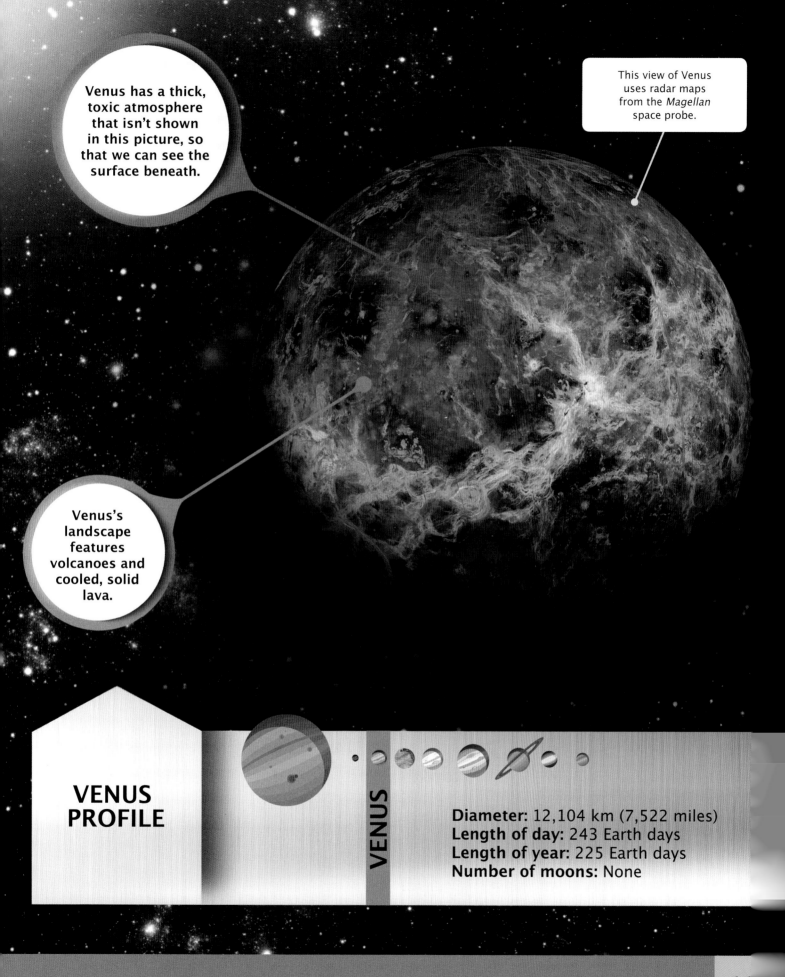

Venus has a thick, toxic atmosphere that isn't shown in this picture, so that we can see the surface beneath.

This view of Venus uses radar maps from the *Magellan* space probe.

Venus's landscape features volcanoes and cooled, solid lava.

VENUS PROFILE

VENUS

Diameter: 12,104 km (7,522 miles)
Length of day: 243 Earth days
Length of year: 225 Earth days
Number of moons: None

Our Planet

Earth is the largest of the solar system's rocky planets, and it is also the one with the most interesting surface. Not only is our home world mostly covered in water, but its surface is always changing through a process called plate tectonics.

World of Water

Earth's orbit around the Sun puts it in a region astronomers call the Goldilocks zone. The temperature across most of the surface is not too hot, not too cold, but "just right" for liquid water. A "water cycle" moves this life-giving chemical between liquid, gas, and solid ice, and helps shape Earth's surface.

Earth's atmosphere acts as a blanket. It protects the planet from extreme temperature changes.

The huge amounts of water on Earth help to explain its abundant life. Water is very important for life, because it allows chemicals and nutrients to move around.

DID YOU KNOW? Water covers **71 percent** of Earth's surface.

EARTH

Diameter: 12,742 km (7,918 miles)
Length of day: 23 h 56 m
Length of year: 365.25 days
Number of moons: One

During the water cycle, water vaporizes (becomes a gas) and rises to make clouds in our atmosphere.

Jigsaw Planet

Earth is made up of layers. At its core is solid ball of iron and nickel, with an inner temperature of 5,400 °C (9,752 °F). Above this lies the mantle, made of molten rock, called magma. Earth's thin outer layer, or crust, is a jigsaw puzzle of giant pieces called plates that float on top of the magma. Over millions of years plates move apart or together, changing the shape and size of the continents and oceans.

crust

mantle

Plates move by a few cm (in) each year.

inner core

outer core

The Moon

Highland areas contain countless ancient craters.

Earth's constant partner, the Moon is the largest natural satellite compared to its planet in our solar system. It is an airless ball of rock covered in craters (bowl-shaped holes) formed when smaller objects smashed into it billions of years ago.

Seas and Highlands

The Moon's surface is a mix of dark, fairly smooth areas called seas or *maria*, and bright, cratered areas called highlands. The seas are what is left over of huge big craters that formed about four billion years ago. They were later flooded and then smoothed out by lava erupting from beneath the surface.

Gravity on the Moon is just one-sixth of Earth's.

Lessons from *Apollo*

Twelve NASA astronauts walked on the surface of the Moon between 1969 and 1972. By studying its rocks and collecting samples they helped us understand the history of the entire solar system—how the planets formed from countless smaller particles crashing together about 4.5 billion years ago. The Moon itself was created when a Mars-sized planet slammed into Earth toward the end of this stage.

MOON PROFILE

Diameter: 3,474 km (2,159 miles)
Distance from Earth: 384,400 km (238,700 miles)
Rotation period: 27.32 Earth days
Length of orbit: 27.32 Earth days

THE MOON

More recent craters spray debris (shards of rock) across the landscape.

Dark seas fill the outlines of large ancient craters.

The first manned Moon landing touched down in the Sea of Tranquility in July 1969.

This radar map shows high areas in yellow and red, and low areas in blue. It clearly shows a huge crater at the Moon's south pole.

DID YOU KNOW? The *Apollo* astronauts brought 381 kg (840 lb) of **Moon rocks** back to Earth.

Mars

The outermost rocky planet is also the one most like Earth. Mars today is a cold desert with thin, toxic air, but the newest discoveries have shown that it used to be much more welcoming, and that it might be again in the future.

Rocks reveal traces of past water.

Desert Planet?

Mars owes its famous red sands to large amounts of iron oxide, better known as rust. But sand dunes are only one part of the varied Martian landscape. Mars is also home to the largest volcano in the solar system (Olympus Mons, which is currently not active), and the deepest canyon, a huge crack in the surface called the Mariner Valley.

Martian Explorers

Mars is the best explored of all the other planets in the solar system. Many countries have sent space probes to map it from orbit, while NASA has landed wheeled rovers on the surface. Together, the different space agencies have shown that large amounts of water used to flow on Mars (it is now locked away as ice in the upper layers of soil). Is it possible there used to be life on this planet?

NASA's *Curiosity* rover has covered more than 15 km (9 miles) of the Martian surface.

MARS PROFILE

Diameter: 6,789 km (4,217 miles)
Length of day: 24 h 37 m
Length of year: 1.88 Earth years
Number of moons: Two

MARS

Two small, lumpy moons called Phobos (left) and Deimos orbit Mars. Astronomers are not sure if they formed alongside Mars, or used to be asteroids.

Bright ice caps at Mars's north and south poles are larger in winter and smaller in summer.

The northern half of the planet is mostly made up of smooth plains.

Air pressure on Mars is less than one percent of Earth's, and the atmosphere is mostly carbon dioxide.

DID YOU KNOW? The Martian moon **Phobos** is falling in a spiral toward the planet. It will smash into it about 50 million years from now.

The Asteroid Belt

Between the orbits of Mars and Jupiter lies a wide region of space where most of the solar system's asteroids orbit. Astronomers think there could be a few hundred millon of these rocky and icy worlds, but they are so spread out that it is easy to pass through the belt.

Where Asteroids Come From

The belt is a region where Jupiter's strong gravity stops small objects grouping together to form bigger ones, so no planet could ever form here. When asteroids do crash into each other, they break into smaller objects. The orbits of these objects spread out to form asteroid "families."

This artist's impression (picture) shows the asteroids much more tightly packed than they are in reality.

Ceres's smooth landscape suggests an icy crust.

Ceres

The largest object in the belt, Ceres, is only one third the diameter of Earth's Moon. It is made from a mix of rock and ice that helps to smooth out its landscape. Experts think there could be a layer of salty water hidden beneath the solid crust. The bright patches in the middle of craters may be caused by this water rising to the surface.

DWARF PLANET PROFILE

Name: Ceres
Diameter: 945 km (587 miles)
Length of day: 0.38 Earth days
Length of year: 4.6 Earth years
Mass: 0.00015 Earths

ASTEROID BELT

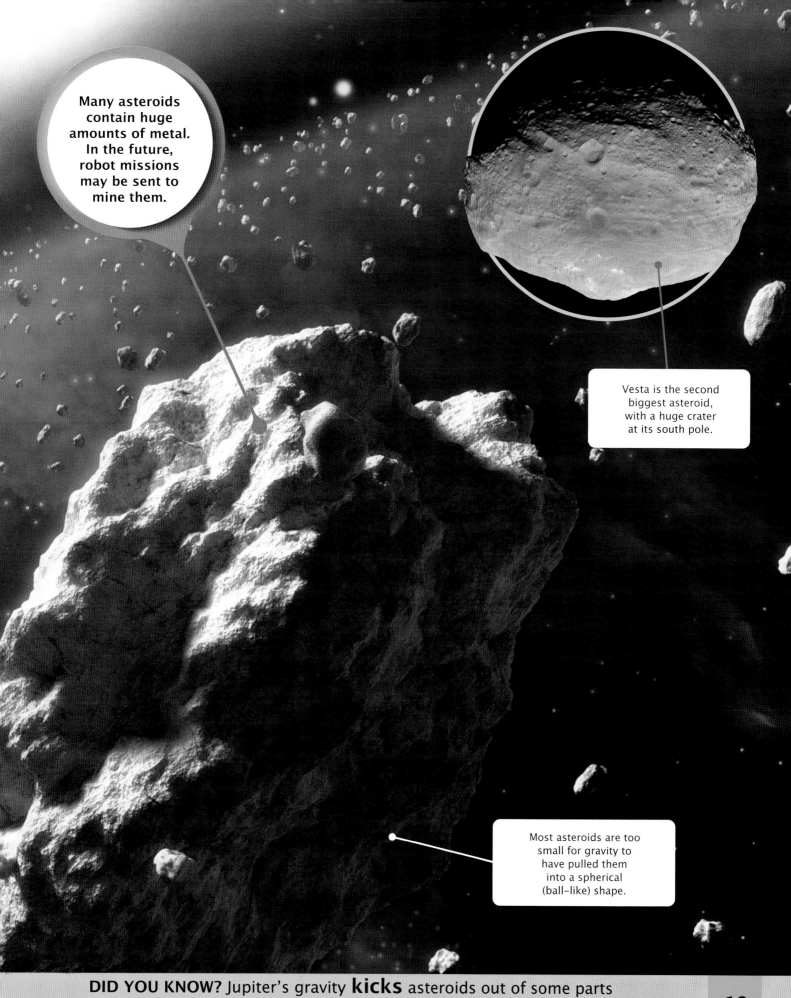

Many asteroids contain huge amounts of metal. In the future, robot missions may be sent to mine them.

Vesta is the second biggest asteroid, with a huge crater at its south pole.

Most asteroids are too small for gravity to have pulled them into a spherical (ball-like) shape.

DID YOU KNOW? Jupiter's gravity **kicks** asteroids out of some parts of the asteroid belt, sometimes into orbits that come closer to Earth.

Jupiter

Named after the ruler of the Roman gods, Jupiter is the largest planet in our solar system. This gas giant is the fifth planet, separated from the four inner, rocky planets by the asteroid belt. Ninety percent of Jupiter's atmosphere is hydrogen gas. Most of the rest is helium.

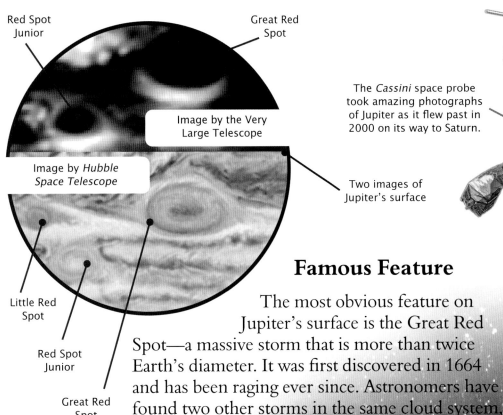

Red Spot Junior

Great Red Spot

Image by the Very Large Telescope

Image by *Hubble Space Telescope*

Little Red Spot

Red Spot Junior

Great Red Spot

The *Cassini* space probe took amazing photographs of Jupiter as it flew past in 2000 on its way to Saturn.

Two images of Jupiter's surface

Famous Feature

The most obvious feature on Jupiter's surface is the Great Red Spot—a massive storm that is more than twice Earth's diameter. It was first discovered in 1664 and has been raging ever since. Astronomers have found two other storms in the same cloud system, nicknamed Red Spot Junior and Little Red Spot.

Ganymede is the largest moon in the solar system.

Moons and Rings

Jupiter has at least 95 moons. The four largest—Io, Europa, Ganymede, and Callisto—can be seen from Earth. They are called the Galilean moons, because the Italian astronomer Galilei was one of the first to describe them. Jupiter is also orbited by thin, dark rings of dust.

PLANET PROFILE

Diameter: 143,000 km (88,800 miles)
Length of day: 9 h 56 m
Length of year: 11.86 Earth years
Number of moons: 95

White bands of cloud are called zones.

Red-brown bands are called belts.

DID YOU KNOW? Jupiter is two-and-a-half times **bigger** than the other solar system planets put together.

Saturn, Uranus, and Neptune

The three giant planets of the outer solar system are all smaller than Jupiter. Saturn is quite similar to Jupiter, but Uranus and Neptune are "ice giants"—beneath their blue-green atmospheres they are mostly a mix of slushy chemicals including water.

Rings

All four giant planets are surrounded by ring systems, but Saturn's are by far the most impressive. They are made up of trillions of icy particles in orbit above the planet's equator. They often crash into each other, which keeps them in orbit.

This is Titan, the largest of Saturn's moons.

Saturn's rings are thousands of miles across, but are very thin.

SATURN PROFILE

Diameter: 116,500 km (72,400 miles)
Length of day: 10 h 33 m
Length of year: 29.46 Earth years
Number of moons: 145

SATURN

DID YOU KNOW? Some astronomers think that Uranus and Neptune might have **swapped** orbits early in the solar system's history.

Uranus has 13 rings and 27 known moons.

World on its Side

Most of the solar system's planets are a little tilted in their orbits around the Sun, but only Uranus is completely knocked over on one side. This makes it look like the planet "rolls" along its orbit. It gives Uranus extreme seasons—at the poles, winter is one long night lasting almost 40 years, followed by a summer of about the same length.

Uranus

Saturn's weather bands are like Jupiter's, but the planet's clouds are surrounded by a creamy haze (fog).

Neptune

Storms on Neptune look like dark spots. High clouds seem white.

Pluto and Beyond

Beyond the orbit of Neptune lies a ring of small frozen worlds called "ice dwarfs." Pluto, the most famous of these, was once called a planet in its own right. Even farther out is the Oort Cloud, a cloud of icy comets at the edge of the solar system.

Jan Oort discovered the the cloud that was later named after him by looking at the shapes and directions of comet orbits.

Mysterious World

Pluto is a mix of rock and ice about half the size of the planet Mercury. Such a small, distant world was thought to be a deep-frozen ball of ice, but when NASA's *New Horizons* probe flew past in 2015, it showed a surprising world that may have been shaped by volcano-like eruptions of ice a long time ago.

The temperature at the surface of Pluto ranges from –218 °C (–360 °F), when it is closest to the Sun, to –240 °C (–400 °F).

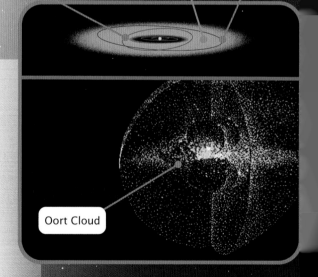

Kuiper Belt

Typical KBO Orbit

Pluto's orbit

Oort Cloud

Kuiper and Oort

The area where ice dwarfs orbit beyond Neptune is called the Kuiper Belt after astronomer Gerard Kuiper. He was one of the first people who thought there was such an area in our solar system. Objects that orbit here are often known as Kuiper Belt Objects (KBOs). From the edge of the Kuiper Belt, the huge Oort Cloud stretches out for almost a light-year, beginning as a broad disk, then opening out into a huge ball of icy, sleeping comets.

DWARF PLANET PROFILE

Diameter: 2,374 km (1,475 miles)
Length of day: 6.39 Earth days
Length of year: 248 Earth years
Number of moons: 5

Pluto's biggest moon, Charon, is more than half the size of Pluto itself.

Pluto's surface is mostly nitrogen, methane, and carbon monoxide ices.

Pluto might have active ice volcanoes even today.

DID YOU KNOW? Pluto is the god of the **underworld** in Greek myths, but the name is also a nod to Percival Lowell (PL), who built the observatory where it was discovered.

Astronomy

A typical person can see about 3,000 stars in the night sky with just their normal eyesight.

Seeing the wonders of space for yourself could not be easier. On a clear, dark night, anyone can stargaze. Special tools such as binoculars or telescopes can help you, but you can also see a lot with nothing more than your eyes.

Ready to Stargaze

To see as much as possible in the night sky, allow your eyes to get used to the dark. If you can, get out into the countryside, away from the glow of nearby cities. Be away from streetlights and phone screens, and do not shine flashlights. After about ten minutes you will find your eyes are much better at seeing faint stars.

Binoculars

If you want to explore more of the night sky, see if you can borrow a pair of binoculars. They are a lot easier to use than a telescope, and you will see thousands more stars than with the naked eye because they pick up more light. They also make everything you view appear larger, so you can see objects such as the Moon in more detail.

Binoculars are an ideal way to get a deeper look at the night sky.

How far can you see without a telescope? All the way to the Andromeda Galaxy, some 2.5 million light-years from Earth!

Many areas of the world are lit up at night. This makes it harder and harder to find really dark skies.

GALAXY PROFILE

Name: Andromeda galaxy
Catalogue number: Messier 31
Constellation: Andromeda
Distance from Earth: 2.5 million light-years
Description: This large spiral galaxy appears as a fuzzy blob of light in dark skies. Binoculars show its oval shape.

DID YOU KNOW? If you need to use a flashlight while stargazing, cover it with red film—your eyes are less sensitive to **red light** so you won't ruin your night vision.

Night and Day

Why is the sky dark at night and light in the daytime? It is all to do with how planet Earth is spinning in space. Half of the world faces toward the Sun at any one time, experiencing daytime, while the other half faces away and has night.

Look east (opposite the sunset) on a clear evening and see if you can spot the dark band of Earth's shadow rising up.

Daytime Skies

Why can't we see stars if we block out our view of the Sun? This is because Earth's atmosphere picks up and "scatters" sunlight from all parts of the sky. It glows a bright blue that drowns out even the brightest stars.

Time Zones

People have always used the movement of the Sun to keep time, but this means that "local time" is different wherever you are on Earth. Faster travel and communication in the 1800s led to the use of time zones. Each zone agrees on a standard time, rather than just using the Sun's position in the sky.

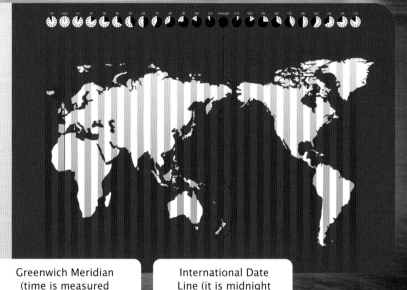

Greenwich Meridian (time is measured from here)

International Date Line (it is midnight here when it is noon on the Greenwich Meridian)

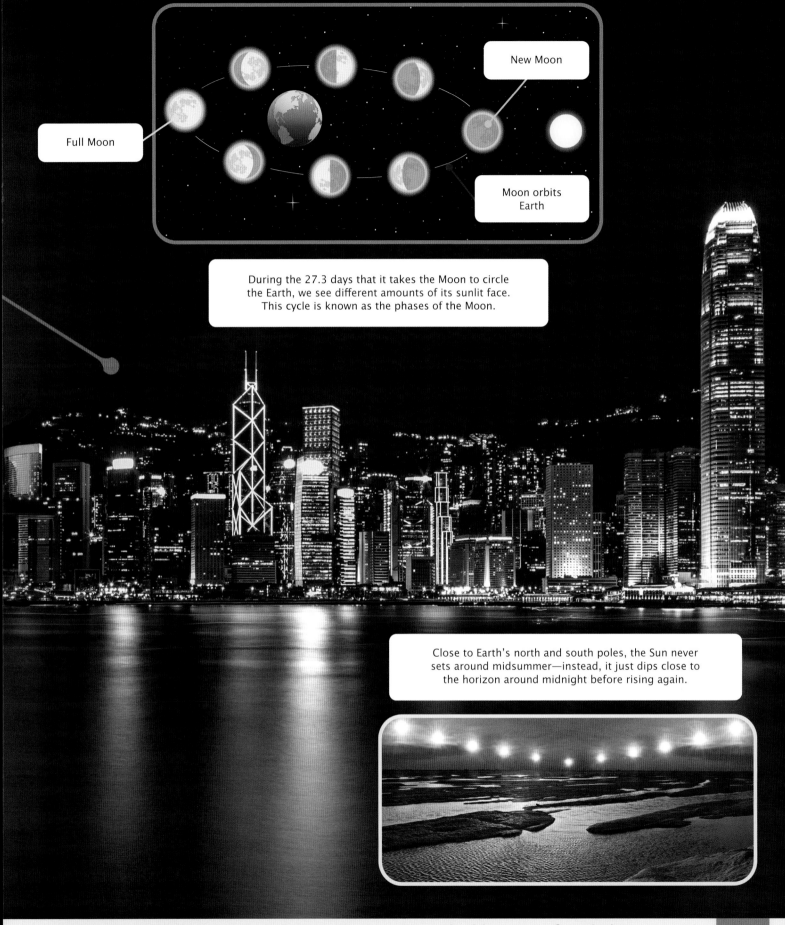

Full Moon

New Moon

Moon orbits
Earth

During the 27.3 days that it takes the Moon to circle
the Earth, we see different amounts of its sunlit face.
This cycle is known as the phases of the Moon.

Close to Earth's north and south poles, the Sun never
sets around midsummer—instead, it just dips close to
the horizon around midnight before rising again.

DID YOU KNOW? Because the atmosphere scatters the blue part of sunlight
away from the Sun itself, the Sun appears to be **yellower** than it actually is.

Earth's Orbit

As Earth orbits the Sun once a year, it goes through a cycle of seasons. This is because the planet is tilted, so the northern and southern hemispheres (halves of Earth) get different amounts of sunlight at different times of year.

Tilted Earth

Earth's axis (an imaginary line that runs through the planet from pole to pole) is tipped at an angle of 23.5 degrees from upright, and points toward the pole star, Polaris. When the Sun also lies in this direction, it is summer in the northern hemisphere, with a high Sun and longer days, while the southern hemisphere has winter. Six months later, it is winter in the north and summer in the south.

Wandering Seasons

Although Earth's axis points toward Polaris at the moment, that isn't always the case. The direction of Earth's tilt slowly wobbles in a 25,800 year cycle called precession, and the cycle of seasons wanders with it. Scientists think this cycle makes a difference to Earth's climate, especially during ice ages when the planet is colder than usual.

In spring, Earth's axis points neither toward nor away from the Sun. Day and night are about the same length, but the days are getting longer.

SPRING

WINTER

SUMMER

AUTUMN

This diagram shows the cycle of seasons in the northern hemisphere.

In summer, one hemisphere tilts toward the Sun. The Sun rises earlier, sets later, and crosses higher in the sky, warming the ground.

In autumn, Earth's axis once again points neither toward nor away from the Sun. Days become shorter and nights get longer.

In winter, one hemisphere tips away from the Sun. It rises later, sets earlier, and has a less warming effect because it crosses lower in the sky.

DID YOU KNOW? Mars, Saturn, and Neptune all have very similar tilts to Earth, so they each go through a similar **cycle** of seasons (though over much longer orbits).

Eclipses

Eclipses are some of the most amazing events in nature. They happen when the Earth, Moon, and Sun line up so that the Moon either passes into Earth's shadow (a lunar eclipse) or passes in front of the Sun (a solar eclipse).

Eclipse Effects

During a lunar eclipse, it is rare for the Moon to disappear completely. More often, it turns a coppery or bloody red as it reflects light that has passed through Earth's atmosphere. Solar eclipses are far more impressive, but they should only ever be watched through special safety glasses.

Conditions in Earth's atmosphere affect the look of an eclipsed Moon.

The last rays of sunlight create an effect called the diamond ring.

Eclipse Myths

Eclipses are rare events, and people around the world have often come up with mythical stories to explain them. The Vikings believed that the Sun was being eaten by wolves, while the ancient Chinese blamed a dragon. Even when most people realized that the Moon was creating the eclipse, many still believed that eclipses could bring bad luck.

DID YOU KNOW? Around 200 BCE, Greek scientist Hipparchus used a solar eclipse to work out the **distance** of the Moon from Earth. He got it right to within ten percent!

During a total solar eclipse, the Sun's outer atmosphere, or corona, can be seen from Earth.

Total solar eclipses last for just a few minutes before the Sun can be seen again.

Partial eclipse

Moon's shadow

Moon

Sun

Total eclipse

Moon's orbit

Earth's shadow

Eclipsed Moon

Earth's orbit

How it Happens

Eclipses only happen because the Sun and Moon look the same size in Earth's sky. This means they need to be exactly lined up for a solar eclipse, which is very rare.

Shooting Stars

Looking into the sky on any dark night, you may see a sudden flash of light—the trail of a shooting star or meteor. This comes from tiny particles of dust burning up as they enter Earth's atmosphere.

Meteor Showers

The space between the planets is full of dust, so shooting stars happen every night. But there are some intense bursts of meteors that happen at the same time each year. These meteor showers happen when Earth crosses a trail of dust particles left behind by a comet.

This drawing shows the Leonid meteor storm of November 1870.

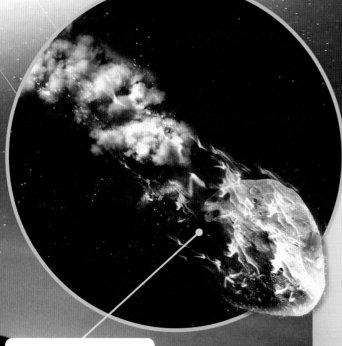

A fireball that exploded over Russia in 2013 shone brighter than the Sun.

Fireballs

A bright meteor that outshines any star is called a fireball. These objects are sometimes too big to burn up in the atmosphere and actually hit the ground. Others end their descent (fall) with a sudden explosion. Bright fireballs can move surprisingly slowly, and are sometimes mistaken for UFOs.

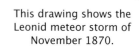

The Leonids are a regular meteor shower that is strongest in a storm that happens about every 30 years.

During a meteor storm, shooting stars can fall like rain.

When Earth crosses a very dense cloud of comet debris, thousands of shooting stars can fall in a meteor storm.

Meteor Calendar

Name	Date	Direction (constellation)
Quadrantids	Early January	Böotes
Lyrids	Mid-April	Lyra
Eta Aquarids	Early May	Aquarius
Arietids	Early June	Aries
Delta Aquarids	July–August	Aquarius
Perseids	Early August	Perseus
Orionids	Mid-October	Orion
Leonids	Mid-November	Leo
Geminids	Mid-December	Gemini

DID YOU KNOW? Bright shooting stars can appear red, yellow, white, or even green depending on the **elements** contained in their dust.

Meteorite Impacts

Space rocks that make it all the way to Earth's surface are called meteorites, and they can cause a lot of damage when they hit the ground. Large meteorites smash craters into Earth's surface, scatter debris across a wide area, and can even change the weather.

Fragments (small pieces) of meteorite found around the Meteor Crater site show that the incoming space rock was rich in iron.

The Moon records impacts (crashes) from up to four billion years ago.

DID YOU KNOW? Much of the world's **nickel** is mined at the site of a large comet impact crater in Ontario, Canada.

Meteorite Hunting

Scientists find meteorites interesting because they are often made of material that has not changed since the early days of the solar system. But unless you see it fall, how do you tell a meteorite from a normal Earth rock? The trick is to look for them where no natural rocks should be—in deserts, or on top of the ice in polar regions.

Scientists in Antarctica collect a meteorite lying on top of the ice.

Damage from a 1908 fireball explosion over Siberia

Meteor Crater in Arizona is about 1,200 m (3,900 ft) wide. It was created when a 50-m (165-ft) meteorite landed about 50,000 years ago.

Dangers from Space

The largest meteorites can cause damage far beyond where they land. They fling fiery debris very far and throw huge amounts of dust into the air, blocking out sunlight. Sixty-five million years ago a huge asteroid impact in Mexico helped to wipe out the dinosaurs.

Lights in the Sky

Earth's atmosphere creates many beautiful light effects that can be seen by day or night. They include rainbow-like haloes around the Sun and Moon and even glowing clouds. The most lovely of all are the northern and southern lights.

Particles from Space

The northern and southern lights (aurorae) are created when particles from the solar wind are pulled into the atmosphere above Earth's poles by our planet's magnetic field. As they hit the air up to 150 km (90 miles) high in the sky, they pass on energy, which means they glow in hues from green to red to blue.

Green glows are created more than 100 km (60 miles) above Earth's surface. These are the most common form of aurora.

A halo forms around the Sun when ice crystals in the atmosphere are bending light (just as water drops create a rainbow).

The Zodiacal Light

One of the most beautiful sky effects is also the most difficult to see. The zodiacal light is a glow caused when dust in the solar system is reflecting sunlight. It stretches through the constellations of the zodiac where the planets are usually seen, but it is very faint and can only be spotted in the darkest, clearest skies.

Aurorae trace the lines of Earth's magnetic field, where solar wind particles are arriving from space.

Northern and southern lights can often be seen in polar regions. They sometimes show in areas a little closer to the equator, too.

Ice crystals in the air create a halo around the Moon.

Icy Glows

In cold weather, ice in Earth's atmosphere can bend light in many different directions, creating haloes around the Sun or Moon, and bright "sundogs" in clouds to the left or right of the Sun. A rarer sight are so-called noctilucent clouds—clouds of ice high in the sky that glow because they catch the sunlight long after the Sun itself has set.

DID YOU KNOW? Rare auroral **storms** can disturb Earth's magnetic field, damaging satellites in orbit and even causing power cuts on the ground!

Comets

Clouds of icy debris orbit the Sun at the edge of the solar system. Normally these objects are invisible, but when a large chunk of ice comes close to the Sun and begins to heat up, the results can be beautiful. The frozen object becomes the heat-filled core, or nucleus, of a spectacular comet.

Comet Appearances

As a comet nucleus warms up, ice starts to melt and escape as jets of gas. These form a glowing atmosphere around it, called the coma. As the comet gets closer to the Sun, radiation (escaping energy) and the solar wind pull at the coma, creating a glowing tail that always points away from the Sun.

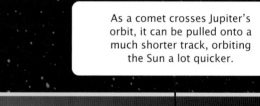

Bright comets can show both a blue gas tail and a yellowish dust tail. The coma, or head of the comet, can easily grow to be larger than Jupiter.

As a comet crosses Jupiter's orbit, it can be pulled onto a much shorter track, orbiting the Sun a lot quicker.

Comets have been seen as signs of bad luck since ancient times. Here, the Aztec king Moctezuma II watches a comet that was believed to show his empire would soon fall.

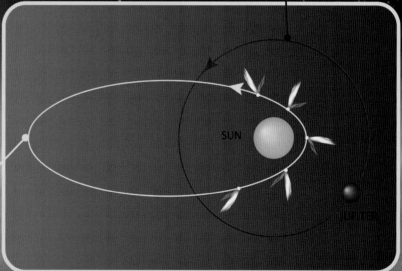

Most comets follow long orbits that only visit the inner solar system every few thousand years.

SUN

JUPITER

DID YOU KNOW? Sightings of comet Halley, which returns to the inner solar system about every 76 years, have been **traced** as far back as 240 BCE.

Exploring Comets

Comets hold deep-frozen material
from the early solar system. This
is one reason why they have
been visited by space probes.
Launched in 2004, *Rosetta* began
to orbit comet 67P in August
2014 and placed a lander on its
surface that November. *Deep
Impact* was launched in January
2005. In July it fired a heavy
"impactor" into the surface of
comet Tempel 1 so that it could
measure the chemistry of the material
that sprayed out.

The Northern Night Sky

In the course of a night, Earth's rotation makes the northern night sky slowly spin around the central pole star, Polaris.

Astronomers split Earth's sky into two hemispheres, or halves, but most people on Earth can see more than half of the sky in a year. People living north of the equator can see all of the northern sky and, depending on where they are, a good amount of the southern sky.

From Earth's north pole, all of the northern sky can be seen.

Northern Stars

The northern sky surrounds Polaris, the pole star that lies directly above Earth's own north pole. Its most famous constellations include Ursa Major (the Great Bear), Leo (the Lion), and Taurus (the Bull). The Milky Way (see page 5) is most visible in the constellation of Cygnus (the Swan), and Virgo (the Maiden) is home to a dense cluster of galaxies.

This old star map shows many of Ptolemy's constellations.

Ancient Constellations

Astronomers split the sky into 88 constellations—areas of the sky marked by a pattern of stars. Forty-eight of these (including most of the northern ones) date back almost 2,000 years to the work of Greek-Egyptian astronomer Ptolemy. His constellations include the even more ancient star patterns of the zodiac, as well as figures from Greek myths such as King Cepheus, Queen Cassiopeia, the hero Perseus, the princess Andromeda, and the winged horse Pegasus.

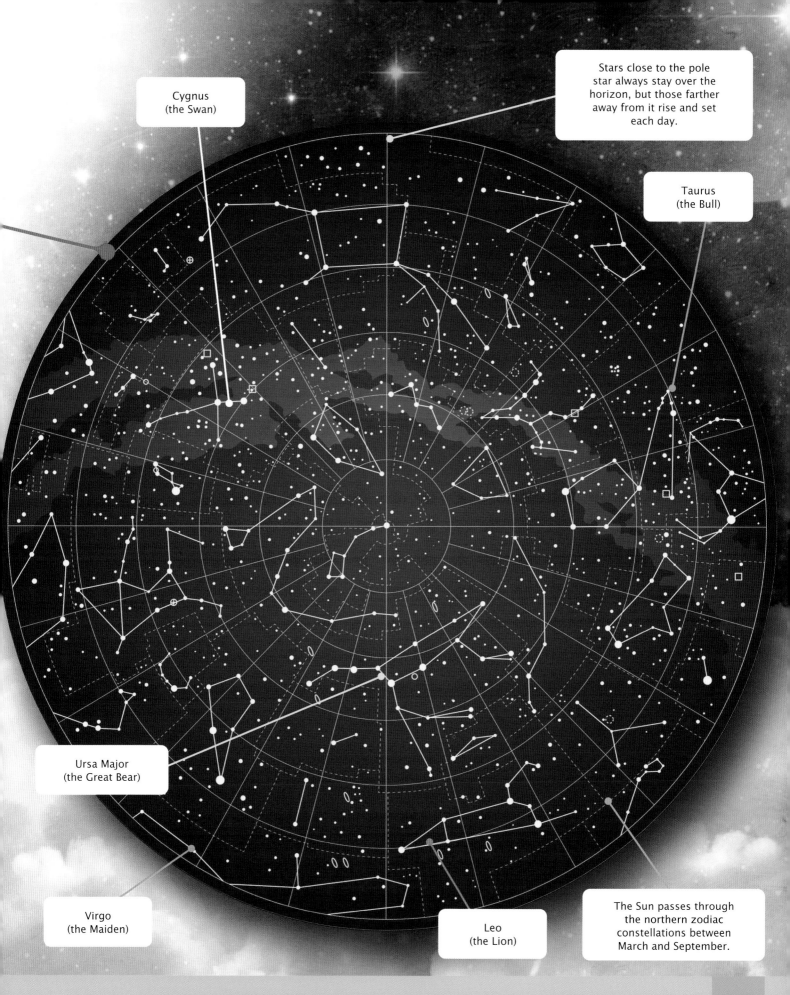

Cygnus
(the Swan)

Stars close to the pole
star always stay over the
horizon, but those farther
away from it rise and set
each day.

Taurus
(the Bull)

Ursa Major
(the Great Bear)

Virgo
(the Maiden)

Leo
(the Lion)

The Sun passes through
the northern zodiac
constellations between
March and September.

DID YOU KNOW? The farther north you live, the **higher** Polaris sits in your sky.

The Southern Night Sky

People living south of the equator can see all of the southern sky and, depending where they are, a good amount of the northern sky. Confusingly, these northern constellations look like they are "upside down" compared to how they are often drawn.

The famous constellation Orion sits on the boundary between northern and southern skies.

Southern Stars

The southern hemisphere is home to the desnest parts of the Milky Way, around the constellations of Sagittarius (the Archer), Centaurus (the Centaur), Carina (the Ship's Keel), and Crux (the Southern Cross). Other famous southern constellations include Scorpius (the Scorpion) and Cetus (the Sea Monster).

This map includes the "southern birds," but was drawn before Lacaille added his constellations.

Later Discoveries

Some southern constellations come from the lists of the Greek-Egyptian astronomer Ptolemy, but most of them are a lot newer. One group, named after birds, was described in the late 1500s by Dutch sailors—the first Europeans to see them. Others were filled in later by French astronomer Nicolas-Louis de Lacaille, who worked in South Africa in the mid-1700s. Most of Lacaille's constellations are named after scientific tools.

DID YOU KNOW? The easiest way to find the pole of the southern sky is to look down the **long arm** of the Southern Cross.

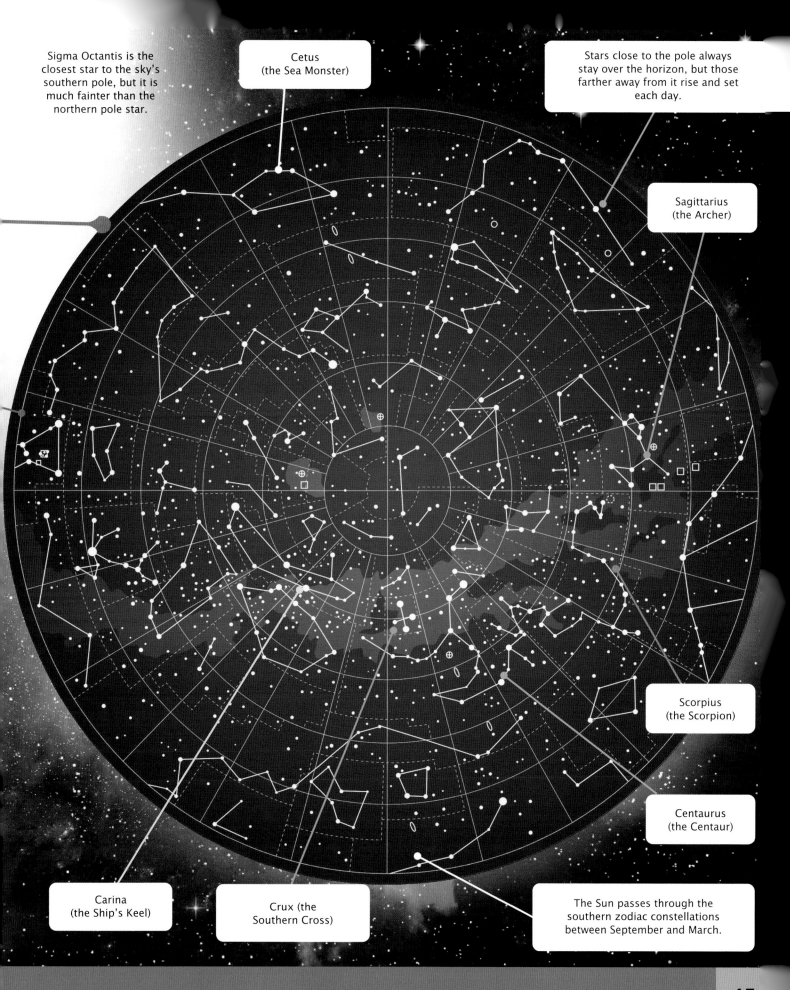

Sigma Octantis is the closest star to the sky's southern pole, but it is much fainter than the northern pole star.

Cetus (the Sea Monster)

Stars close to the pole always stay over the horizon, but those farther away from it rise and set each day.

Sagittarius (the Archer)

Scorpius (the Scorpion)

Centaurus (the Centaur)

Carina (the Ship's Keel)

Crux (the Southern Cross)

The Sun passes through the southern zodiac constellations between September and March.

Space

Solar panels fitted to the service module make electricity in space. The service module is behind the crew capsule.

Outer space is not far away—in fact, it starts just 100 km (60 miles) above your head. That is where scientists and pilots place the "edge of space"—the region where Earth's air fades away to nothing, and where people need spacesuits and spacecraft to survive.

Outside Earth's atmosphere, conditions switch suddenly between freezing darkness and blazing sunlight.

Weightless in Orbit

Most spacecraft and astronauts work in a region called Low Earth Orbit (LEO), where they fly around our planet at a fast enough speed to cancel out the downward pull of Earth's gravity. This means that astronauts on board an orbiting spacecraft float around in weightless conditions, free from the effects of gravity.

Spacecraft operate in an airless type of space called a vacuum.

Astronaut Chris Hadfield relaxes on board the *International Space Station*, which is in LEO.

SPACECRAFT PROFILE

Name: *Orion*
Crewed launch: 2024
Height: 3.3 m (11 ft)
Diameter: 5 m (16 ft)
Weight: 25,800 kg (57,000 lb)
Crew size: 4 people
Launch vehicle: NASA SLS

Crew module protects up to four astronauts from the dangers of space.

Orion flew on its first unmanned test launch in 2014.

Lost in Space

Early spacecraft did not get far enough away from Earth to see our whole planet afloat in space. The first people to do this were the crew of *Apollo 8*, who flew all the way to the Moon and back in December 1968. The pictures they took showed for the first time how tiny and fragile our planet is, and moved people to start taking better care of it.

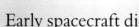

Images taken in space are used to study Earth's changing climate.

NASA's *Orion* spacecraft is made to carry astronauts into Earth's orbit and to nearby space objects.

DID YOU KNOW? The *Orion* spacecraft may one day form part of the first mission to put people on **Mars**.

Early Ideas

People have looked up at the stars and planets, and tried to explain them, since before written history. Many believed that these strange lights in the sky could control events on Earth, and they tried to foresee their movements. This was the birth of astronomy.

Greek Astronomers

The ancient Greeks were the first people to come up with complete models of the Universe, in the last few centuries BCE. Believing that Earth was the biggest and most important object, they put it in the middle of space, with everything else moving around it.

Native peoples of Central and South America built huge stone temples in places that lined them up with the stars and planets in the night sky.

The Greek astronomer Hipparchus realized that the Earth was tilted on its axis.

DID YOU KNOW? A Greek astronomer called **Aristarchus** suggested the Earth goes round the Sun as early as 250 BCE.

Before the invention of telescopes, astronomers used instruments such as this armillary sphere.

A Solar System

The idea of Earth in the middle of everything lasted almost 2,000 years, even though astronomers found it did not help them work out the movement of planets. In 1514, Polish priest Nicolaus Copernicus suggested that the Sun was actually at the heart of our solar system, and Earth was just one of many planets moving around it.

Armillary sphere helps to measure where objects are in the sky.

Copernicus's ideas were not proven until the early 1600s.

Most of the zodiac constellations are animals.

Signs of the Zodiac

Ancient astronomers made pictures out of the stars in the sky—the patterns that we call constellations. They soon noticed that the Sun and planets followed paths around the sky that moved through just 12 of these constellations, so they gave these special importance. They became the signs of the zodiac.

Telescopes

Telescopes are the most important tools astronomers use to look at objects in space. They gather up much more light than our human eyes so that we can see fainter objects, and they create a magnified (blown-up) image so that we can see much smaller details.

Two Designs

Telescopes come in two types. Refractors use two or more lenses at either end of a long tube to create a magnified image. Reflectors use a mirror to reflect light to a lens, and can have a more compact design. The job of the first lens or mirror is to collect light from a large area and bend or reflect it so that it passes through the smaller eyepiece lens.

The Yerkes Observatory refractor is the world's largest successful lens-based telescope.

Birth of the Telescope

The first telescopes were made by Dutch lensmakers around 1608, but the invention was made famous by Italian astronomer Galileo Galilei, who built his own telescope a few months later. He used it to make important discoveries, studying moons around Jupiter, craters on the Moon, and star clouds in the Milky Way.

Galilei's studies made him believe that the planets move around the Sun, as Copernicus had suggested.

DID YOU KNOW? Galilei's first telescope could only magnify by three times.

TELESCOPE PROFILE

Name: Yerkes refractor
Built: 1897
Lens diameter: 102 cm (40 in)
Length: 19.2 m (63 ft)
Weight: 23.5 tonnes (26 tons)
Location: Williams Bay, Wisconsin, U.S.A.

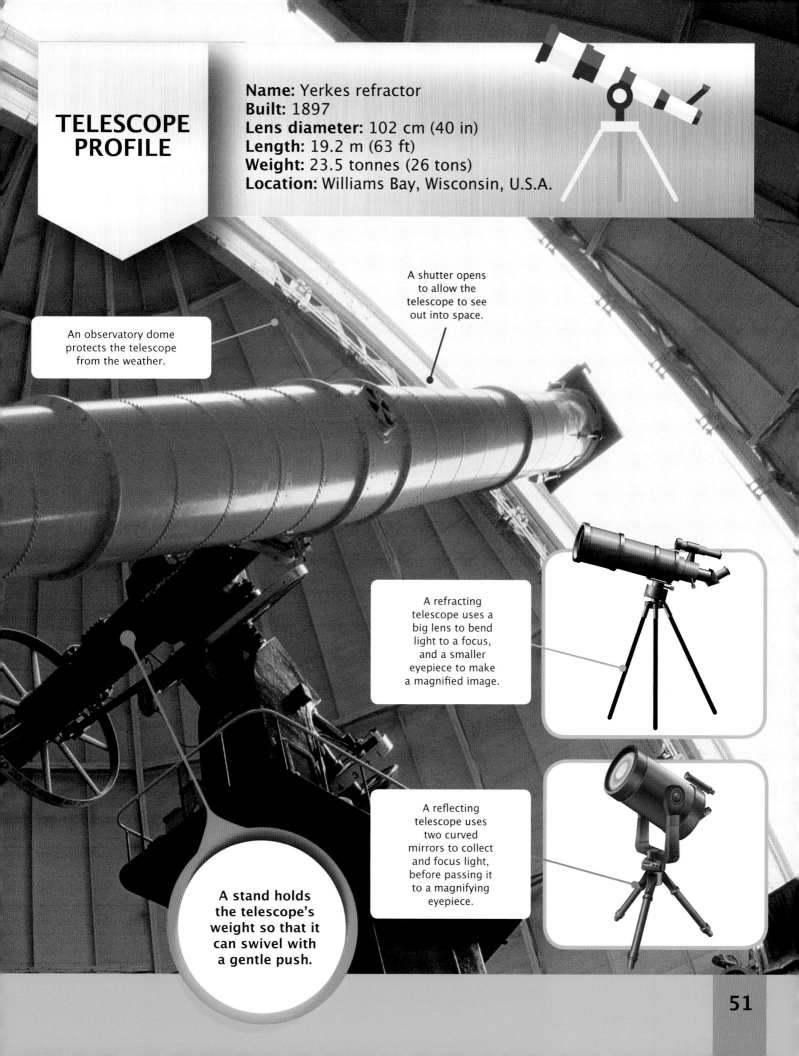

A shutter opens to allow the telescope to see out into space.

An observatory dome protects the telescope from the weather.

A refracting telescope uses a big lens to bend light to a focus, and a smaller eyepiece to make a magnified image.

A reflecting telescope uses two curved mirrors to collect and focus light, before passing it to a magnifying eyepiece.

A stand holds the telescope's weight so that it can swivel with a gentle push.

Giant Telescopes

Today's largest telescopes are all reflectors. They use huge mirrors to collect enormous amounts of light, but astronomers don't look through them directly—instead of an eyepiece, they direct their light into electronic detectors that can reveal any hidden details.

Many Mirrors

Instead of using a single mirror, many modern telescopes use many hexagonal (six-sided) mirror pieces, set together in a honeycomb pattern. Their position and shape can be changed by computer-controlled motors as the telescope swings to look in different directions. A single mirror might bend out of shape under its own weight.

The Canada-France-Hawaii Telescope (CFHT) has a single 3.6-m (11.8-ft) mirror. Its camera takes some of the largest pictures of the sky.

Today's large telescopes are built on high mountains that put them above most of Earth's weather and atmosphere.

The back of the Keck Telescope shows its many mirrors.

TELESCOPE PROFILE

Name: Gemini Telescopes
Built: 1999 and 2000
Mirror diameters: 8.2 m (26.9 ft)
Mirror weights: 20 tonnes (22 tons)
Locations: Mauna Kea, Hawaii and Cerro Pachon, Chile.

Gemini North is an 8.2-m (26.9-ft) telescope in Hawaii. It has an identical twin, Gemini South, in Chile.

Vents in the dome help to keep the telescope cool during the day.

The ELT's mirror is made up of 798 hexagonal segments.

Under Construction

Future telescopes will dwarf even today's monsters. When complete in 2027, the Extremely Large Telescope (ELT) will have a mirror that is an incredible 39.3 m (129 ft) across.

The Electromagnetic Spectrum

Scientists call the light we see with our eyes a form of electromagnetic radiation—a pattern of electric and magnetic waves moving through space at the speed of light. Light is just one small part of a much wider electromagnetic spectrum, and different objects release different kinds of radiation.

Wavelength and Frequency

All kinds of electromagnetic radiation move at the speed of light—the differences between them are because of their wavelength (the length of individual waves) and frequency (the number of waves that pass a fixed point every second). The shorter the wavelength and higher the frequency, the more energy a wave can carry.

The wavelength of red light is almost twice as long as that of blue light.

Planets "shine" by reflecting the light of their stars. The wavelength they reflect can show the chemistry of their atmospheres.

Hot gas clouds in space (called nebulae) release light with wavelengths that link to the mix of gases they are made of.

DID YOU KNOW? When raindrops act like tiny prisms to split up the different wavelengths of sunlight, the result is a **rainbow.**

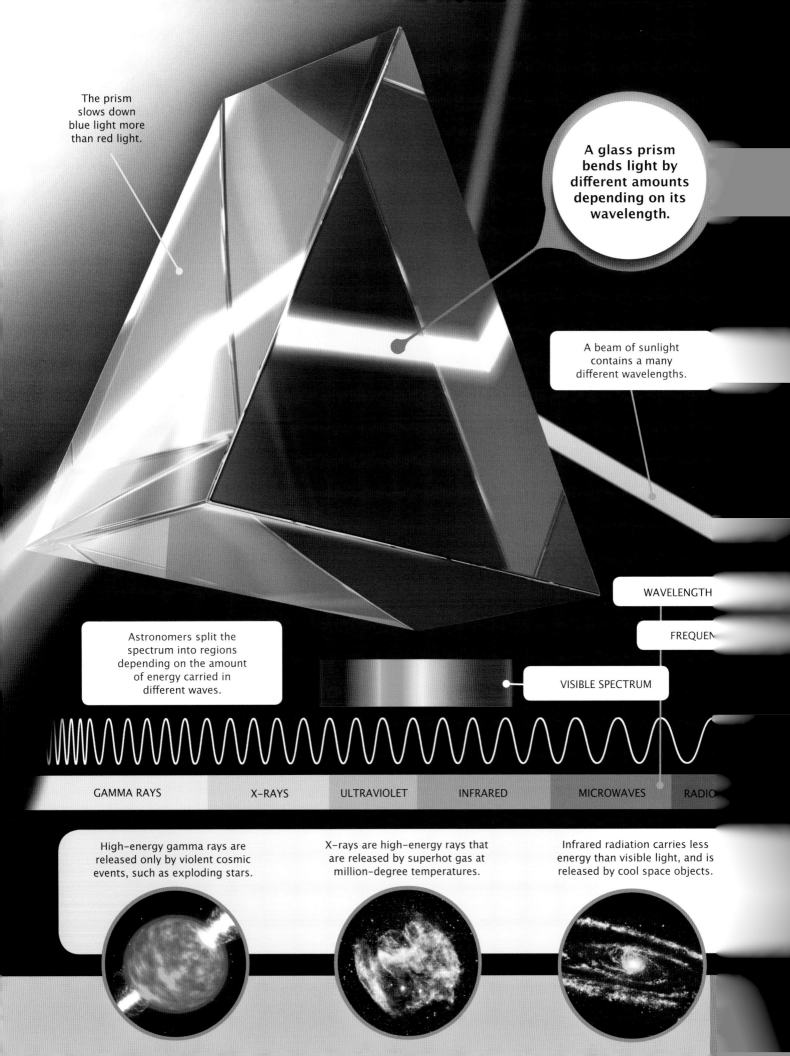

The prism slows down blue light more than red light.

A glass prism bends light by different amounts depending on its wavelength.

A beam of sunlight contains a many different wavelengths.

Astronomers split the spectrum into regions depending on the amount of energy carried in different waves.

WAVELENGTH

FREQUEN

VISIBLE SPECTRUM

GAMMA RAYS   X-RAYS   ULTRAVIOLET   INFRARED   MICROWAVES   RADIO

High-energy gamma rays are released only by violent cosmic events, such as exploding stars.

X-rays are high-energy rays that are released by superhot gas at million-degree temperatures.

Infrared radiation carries less energy than visible light, and is released by cool space objects.

Infrared Telescopes

Objects that are too cold to shine in visible light can still send out a lot of infrared or heat radiation. Almost everything on Earth glows in the infrared, but so do other planets, and the clouds of gas and dust from which stars are born.

Finding Infrared

In order to find the faint infrared radiation from distant space objects, astronomers need to try to block out all the radiation from Earth and even from the telescope itself. This is why infrared telescopes are built on high, cold mountaintops or—even better—launched into space as satellites.

Discovery by Accident

Infrared was the first invisible radiation to be discovered, in 1800. It was found by chance by astronomer William Herschel, during an experiment to measure the temperatures of blue, yellow, and red sunlight. Herschel split light through a prism into a rainbow-like spectrum, but discovered that the temperature was hottest just beyond the red end of this spectrum, where no light can be seen.

As well as infrared, William Herschel is famous for discovering the planet Uranus in 1781.

Winds from newborn stars blow the gas around.

DID YOU KNOW? The *Spitzer Space Telescope* was chilled throughout its mission using **liquid helium**, one of the coldest substances known.

Spitzer Space Telescope view of the Omega Nebula.

An infrared view shows a great number of newborn stars hidden inside the Eagle Nebula's towers of gas and dust.

Red areas show warmer dust, and green and white parts of the picture show hot gas.

Dark lines of cold dust in front of glowing gas.

TELESCOPE PROFILE

Name: _Spitzer Space Telescope_
Launch date: 2003
Mirror diameter: 85 cm (33 in)
Length: 88 m (289 ft)
Weight: 884 kg (1,939 lb)
Operating temperature: −268 °C (−450 °F)

Radio Astronomy

Radio waves are the longest, lowest-energy type of electromagnetic radiation, released by some of the coldest objects in the Universe. They help astronomers to find clouds of hydrogen that shape our galaxy and others.

Giant Dishes

Radio wavelengths are millions of times longer than visible light—so spread out that it is hard to work out where they are coming from. So astronomers build giant radio telescopes—metal dishes that collect waves across a huge surface before measuring them with sensitive electronics.

The Very Large Array in New Mexico combines the signals from 27 dishes to create radio pictures of the sky.

Biggest Dishes

The largest single-dish radio telescope used to be an enormous 300-m (1,000-ft) instrument at Arecibo in Puerto Rico. This huge "detector horn" was hung from cables high above the dish. In 2016, Arecibo was overtaken by FAST, an even larger telescope at Dawodang in southern China. It is an amazing 500 m (1,600 ft) across.

The Arecibo Telescope in Puerto Rico

TELESCOPE PROFILE

Name: Very Large Array
Built: 1973-80
Location: Socorro, New Mexico, U.S.A.
Number of dishes: 27
Dish diameter: 25 m (82 ft) each
Weight: 209,000 kg (460,000 lb) each
Track length: 3 x 21 km (13 miles)

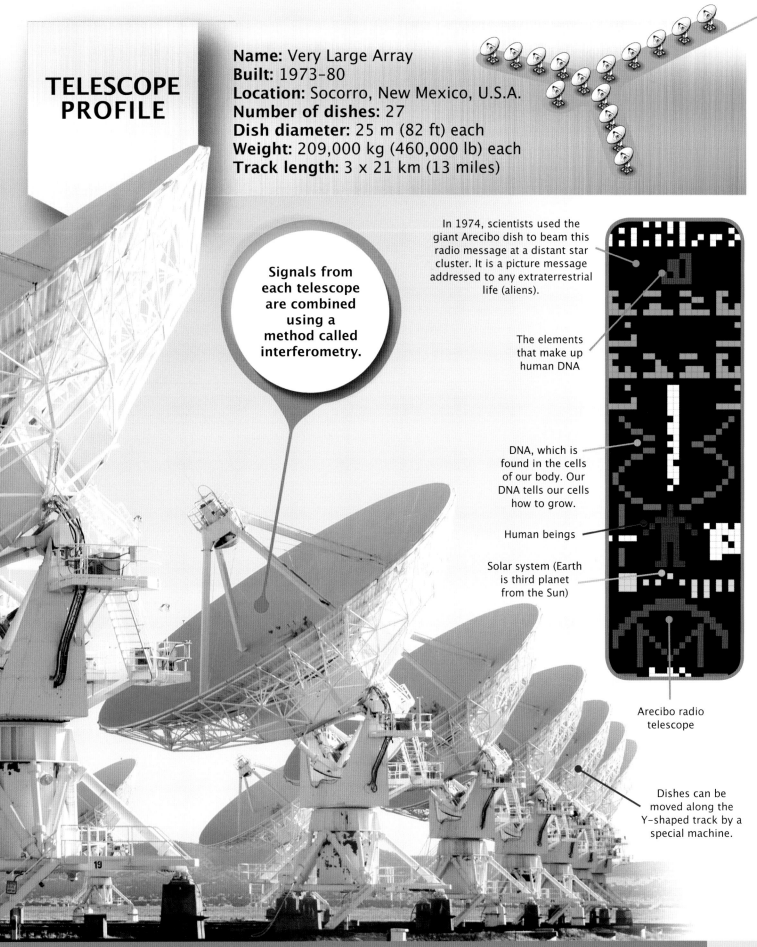

Signals from each telescope are combined using a method called interferometry.

In 1974, scientists used the giant Arecibo dish to beam this radio message at a distant star cluster. It is a picture message addressed to any extraterrestrial life (aliens).

The elements that make up human DNA

DNA, which is found in the cells of our body. Our DNA tells our cells how to grow.

Human beings

Solar system (Earth is third planet from the Sun)

Arecibo radio telescope

Dishes can be moved along the Y-shaped track by a special machine.

DID YOU KNOW? The **Arecibo message** is on its way to a star cluster some 25,000 light-years away, so it could be 50,000 years until we get a reply!

Special Rays

Electromagnetic waves with more energy than visible light are mostly stopped by Earth's atmosphere. This is good for life on Earth, because these rays can be dangerous to humans and animals. But it is a problem for astronomers.

Types of Ray

There are three types of high-energy rays. Those closest to visible light are called ultraviolet (UV) rays, and are released by many objects including the Sun. Those with higher energy are called X-rays and gamma rays. These are created only by the hottest objects and most violent events in the Universe.

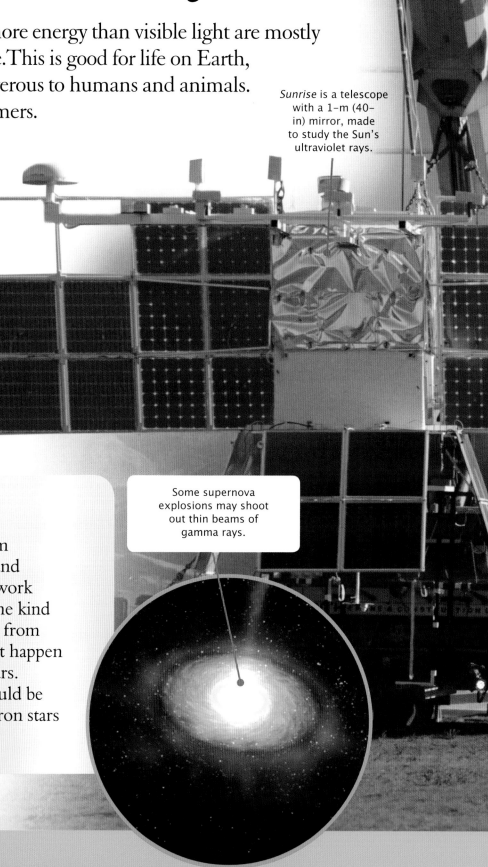

Sunrise is a telescope with a 1-m (40-in) mirror, made to study the Sun's ultraviolet rays.

Some supernova explosions may shoot out thin beams of gamma rays.

Gamma-Ray Bursts

The strongest gamma rays from space come in sudden bursts, and astronomers are still trying to work out where they come from. One kind of gamma-ray burst may come from huge supernova explosions that happen during the death of massive stars. Other, much shorter bursts could be created when superdense neutron stars or black holes come together.

A helium-filled weather balloon lifted *Sunrise* more than 30 km (19 miles) high, where a lot of UV hasn't been stopped by Earth's atmosphere yet.

The *Sunrise* UV telescope is strapped to a balloon. It carried out two missions, in June 2009 and June 2013.

Solar panel makes energy to power the telescope.

X-rays from the Sun reflected off the Moon.

Both *Sunrise* missions were launched from the Esrange Space Center in northern Sweden. It is in the Arctic Circle where, during summertime, the Sun never sets.

DID YOU KNOW? Some scientists believe a gamma-ray burst close by meant that a lot of **life on Earth** got destroyed about 450 million years ago.

Hubble Space Telescope

The most successful telescope ever built, the *Hubble Space Telescope* (*HST*) was the first large visible-light telescope ever put into space. From where it is above Earth's atmosphere, it has the clearest and sharpest views of the Universe.

HST has four bays for carrying many different cameras and other measuring instruments.

Radio antennae connect *HST* with its controllers on Earth using other satellites.

A special tube keeps the mirror safe from direct sunlight and extreme temperature changes.

Hubble has been repaired and upgraded by five space shuttle missions during its lifetime. The last was in 2009.

DID YOU KNOW? People first thought about putting a telescope in space in **1923.**

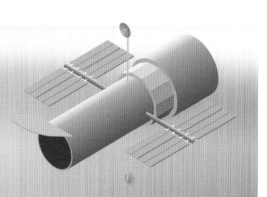

TELESCOPE PROFILE

Name: *Hubble Space Telescope*
Launch date: 1990
Mirror diameter: 2.4 m (7.9 ft)
Length: 13.2 m (43.5 ft)
Weight: 11,110 kg (24,500 lb)

Clever Design

Sent into space in 1990, the *Hubble Space Telescope* is still working with up-to-date technology more than 30 years later. This is because it has a flexible design, with instrument units that can be replaced (removed, so that a newer unit can take its place) and upgraded. The telescope was named after the American astronomer Edwin Hubble.

An astronaut replaces one of *HST*'s instruments.

Solar panels make 1,200 watts of electricity to power the telescope and its instruments.

Discoveries

The *Hubble Space Telescope* has made many important discoveries. It has shown how stars are born in close-up for the first time, helped to discover some of the biggest stars and most distant galaxies in the Universe, and measured the speed at which our Universe is expanding (growing larger). Above all, it has taken amazing images that have forever changed the way we see space.

A *Hubble* image of the Arches, a giant star cluster near the middle of the Milky Way.

Space Observatories

The *HST* is the most famous space telescope, but there are many others. Earth's atmosphere blocks out almost all radiation apart from visible light and radio waves, so if astronomers want to study the Universe at these other wavelengths, they need to do it from orbit.

Benefits and Problems

Nearly all kinds of radiation can be measured better from outside Earth's atmosphere. Space telescopes can collect huge amounts of information. However, being so far from Earth is also a problem. When space telescopes break down, they are usually just left. The *HST* is the only telescope in orbit that has been repaired with the help of a service mission.

Staring at the Stars

Another good thing about having telescopes in orbit is that they do not have to stop observing during daytime. This was useful for *Kepler*, a NASA satellite launched in 2009 to search for planets around other stars. *Kepler*'s camera was designed to watch a single star cloud in the constellation Cygnus non-stop for many years. It was looking for the dips in starlight that happen if a planet passes in front of its star. This mission could only be carried out in space.

So that it can stay pointing in the same direction in space, *Kepler* orbits the Sun rather than the Earth.

A huge sun shield protects the *JWST*'s main mirror.

The *James Webb Space Telescope* (*JWST*) is the biggest telescope ever put into space.

The 18 peces of gold-coated mirror unfolded once the telescope reached orbit.

Temperatures on the underside reach 85 °C (185 °F).

TELESCOPE PROFILE

Name: *James Webb Space Telescope*
Launch date: 25 December 2021
Mirror diameter: 6.5 m (21 ft)
Length: 21.2 m (69.5 ft)
Weight: 6,200 kg (13,600 lb)
Operating temperature: −223 to −266 °C (−389 to −447 °F)

DID YOU KNOW? Some **high-energy rays** are so powerful that they pass straight through traditional telescope mirrors.

Rockets

Rising into space on a jet of flames, rockets need an explosive chemical reaction to push them through Earth's atmosphere. They are noisy, wasteful, and expensive, but they are still the best way of reaching orbit around the Earth.

Stage by Stage

Most rockets are made up of many "stages," each with their own fuel tanks and rocket engines. These stages may be stacked on top of each other, or sit side by side. Only the top stage reaches orbit with its cargo—the burnt-out lower stages fall back to Earth and are usually destroyed.

A rocket stage is mostly made of fuel tanks and engines. Only a small cargo on the top reaches space.

Booster stages help to raise the speed of the top stage and cargo before falling back to Earth.

NASA's Space Launch System will carry the *Orion* spacecraft (pages 46–47) into orbit.

The *V–2* was a rocket with explosive cargo, used as a weapon during World War II. Most modern rockets are based on the *V–2*.

SPACECRAFT PROFILE

Name: *Saturn V*
Launch dates: 1967–73
Total launches: 13
Height: 110.6 m (363 ft)
Diameter: 10.1 m (33 ft)
Weight: 2.29 million kg (5.04 million lb)

DID YOU KNOW? For more than 50 years, the *Saturn V* rocket that took astronauts to the Moon in 1969 was the **biggest rocket** ever built.

Action and Reaction

Rockets rely on a rule that the English scientist Isaac Newton worked out in 1687: "For every action, there is an equal and opposite reaction." This means that the force of exploding gases coming from a rocket engine is always the same as the reaction: the force pushing the engine itself in the opposite direction. The rocket pushes against itself, not the air around it, so it can work even in space, where there is no air.

Isaac Newton discovered the principle of the rocket.

First stage with four rocket engines

Pioneers

The first satellites and astronauts were launched during the "space race," a time of competition between the United States and Russia. Both sides made huge breakthroughs while they each tried to beat the other country and complete many space "firsts."

Gagarin was a trained test pilot, but he wasn't given a lot of control over his spacecraft.

Russian astronaut Yuri Gagarin became the first man in space during the *Vostok 1* mission on 12 April 1961.

DID YOU KNOW? The first woman in space, **Valentina Tereshkova,** flew on *Vostok 6* in June 1963.

Race to the Moon

The Soviet Union (a group of countries with Russia) put the first satellite in space in 1957, and the first man in space four years later. The United States found it hard to catch up. It ended up winning the space race thanks to its Apollo missions, which landed the first astronauts on the Moon in July 1969.

American astronaut Neil Armstrong was the first person to step onto the Moon.

Laika's Story

After the successful launch of the *Sputnik 1* satellite in October 1957, Russian politicians ordered their engineers to work on a new "spectacular." The answer was *Sputnik 2*, a much larger satellite that carried a living passenger—Laika. This small dog had been picked up as a stray and specially trained. Sadly, Laika died from stress and overheating shortly after launch.

Laika was the first animal to orbit the Earth.

SPACECRAFT PROFILE

Name: *Vostok 1*
Launch date: 12 April 1961
Diameter: 2.3 m (7.5 ft)
Flight duration: 108 minutes
Orbits: 1
Launch site: Baikonur, now in Kazakhstan
Crew: Yuri Gagarin

The Space Shuttle

After the end of the space race, the U.S. space agency NASA started working on a new kind of spacecraft—a reusable spaceplane to make space travel more common. Although it completed some amazing missions, the space shuttle didn't get used as much as hoped, and it was retired in 2011.

Shuttle Launch

The space shuttle system was made up of a plane-like "orbiter" vehicle with a large cargo hold and rocket engines on its tail. It launched into orbit fuelled by a huge external (outside) tank, and helped out by two strap-on booster rockets. These boosters fell away during takeoff but could be found and reused.

The shuttle blasts off from Launch Complex 39 at NASA's Kennedy Space Center.

Gliding back to Earth

After finishing its mission, the shuttle orbiter dropped back into Earth's atmosphere in a fiery process called re-entry. When it was back in the atmosphere, the shuttle moved like a giant high-speed glider, heading for a landing strip in either California or Florida, U.S.A.. When it touched down at a speed of about 343 km/h (213 mph), the tail part release parachutes that helped the wheel brakes to stop the shuttle.

Black tiles on the underside of the shuttle were designed to shield it from the heat of re-entry. They didn't work during *Columbia*'s 2003 re-entry, which meant that the shuttle broke up.

Large cargo bay carried satellites into orbit or was used as research space.

The shuttle could change its direction in orbit using small rocket motors placed around its body.

Challenger exploded after launch in 1986. It was one of two shuttles lost in flight; seven astronauts died in each accident.

Booster rockets and main engines fired together during launch.

USA

SPACECRAFT PROFILE

Name: Space shuttle
Launch dates: 1981–2011
Total launches: 135
Height: 56.1 m (184.2 ft)
Weight: 68,600 kg (151,200 lb)
Crew size: 3–6 people
Orbiting speed: 28,800 km/h (17,895.5 mph)

DID YOU KNOW? There were five working **space shuttles** in total (*Columbia, Challenger, Discovery, Atlantis,* and *Endeavour*), plus a prototype called *Enterprise.*

Launchpads

Sending rockets and their cargo into space is a dangerous and noisy business. Space agencies build large, specialized launch areas that are a long way from where people live.

Fuel is not pumped into the tanks until the rocket is in position on the launchpad.

At Baikonur, Kazakhstan, rockets are moved around on huge trains. They are only stood upright when they reach the launchpad.

Russia has used the *Soyuz* rocket since the 1960s.

Launch towers lock into place around the rocket and release during takeoff.

DID YOU KNOW? *Soyuz* rockets at **Baikonur** are still launched from the same pad that launched Yuri Gagarin's *Vostok 1* in 1961.

Mission Controllers

Rocket launches are watched from a control room inside the launch area. Not long after the rocket has safely left the pad, control passes to a separate mission control room that may be far away. For example, NASA's mission control at Houston, Texas, is more than a thousand miles from its launchpads at Cape Canaveral, Florida.

Experts check different parts of the spacecraft's systems from their desks.

Escape rocket system pulls crew capsule away from the main rocket in an emergency.

Floating Launchpad

Sea Launch is a company that offers rocket launches from a floating platform called *Ocean Odyssey.* By placing the platform close to the equator in the Pacific Ocean, rockets can use the speed boost from the Earth's rotation. Missions are cheaper because they use less fuel and can carry heavier cargo. Launching at sea also means there is a smaller risk of rockets falling back on areas where there are people.

Sea Launch's command ship and launch platform.

SPACECRAFT PROFILE

Name: *Soyuz* rocket
Launch dates: 1966-present
Total launches: 1,700+
Height: 49.5 m (162.4 ft) in current version
Weight: 305,000 kg (672,000 lb)

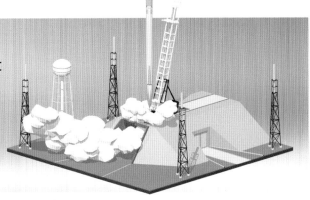

Astronaut Training

Only a few hundred people have gone into space until now, and most of them had years of training before their launch. Some astronauts are specialist pilots, and many are scientists or engineers.

In the Tank

Sometimes an astronaut will need to do difficult work while he or she is weightless and wearing a bulky spacesuit. The best way to train for this on Earth is in a special water tank. Astronauts wear a suit designed for training and use dummy tools for practice. Divers watch over them.

Space Tourists

Not all astronauts are professionals (trained experts). Since the 1990s, Russia has given wealthy space fans the chance to make short trips into orbit—if they can pay a few million dollars toward the costs of the *Soyuz* rocket. These space tourists still go through many months of training, however—if only to make sure they don't get in the way of the professionals!

Astronauts use special tools that work through bulky gloves.

NASA's Neutral Buoyancy Laboratory at Houston, Texas, has one of the world's largest diving tanks.

An air bag helps to make sure the astronaut is floating without rising or sinking. This is called neutral buoyancy.

Dummy space station pieces are used to learn how to build in space.

English scientist Stephen Hawking flew on a reduced–gravity plane in 2007.

Floating or Falling?

Astronauts and others can enjoy feeling weightless for a short time by flying on a reduced-gravity aircraft. These planes fly up to great heights before diving at a speed that is the same as the pull of Earth's gravity. As people and objects on board fall at the same speed as the plane, they are in zero gravity for up to 25 seconds at a time.

DID YOU KNOW? The **Neutral Buoyancy Laboratory** pool holds 23,500 kl (6.2 million gallons) of water.

Early Space Stations

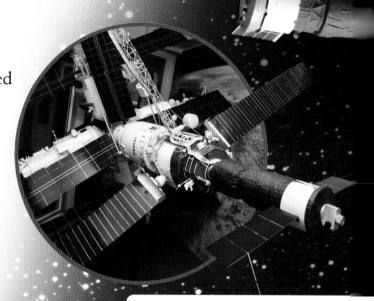

The inside of *Mir* became cluttered and messy over the years.

A space station is a base that is in orbit around the Earth, where astronauts can live and work for weeks or even months. The first stations were launched by Russia and the United States in the 1970s, and Russia carried on building them and improving their designs for the next 20 years.

Record-Breakers

From 1971, Russia launched a series of seven stations called *Salyut*. NASA, meanwhile, launched a single station called *Skylab*, which was visited by three crews in 1973–74. From 1986, Russia built *Mir*, an orbital laboratory with a few different modules (units) for living and working. Russian astronauts working on *Mir* set a number of records including the first person to spend a year in space.

A Russian *Soyuz* unit attached to *Mir* was used as a lifeboat by the crew in emergencies.

SPACECRAFT PROFILE

Name: *Skylab*
Launch date: 14 May 1973
Width: 17 m (55.8 ft)
Length: 25.1 m (82.4 ft)
Completed missions: 3
Crew size: 3 people per mission
Re-entry: 11 July 1979 (burnt up and crashed in Western Australia)

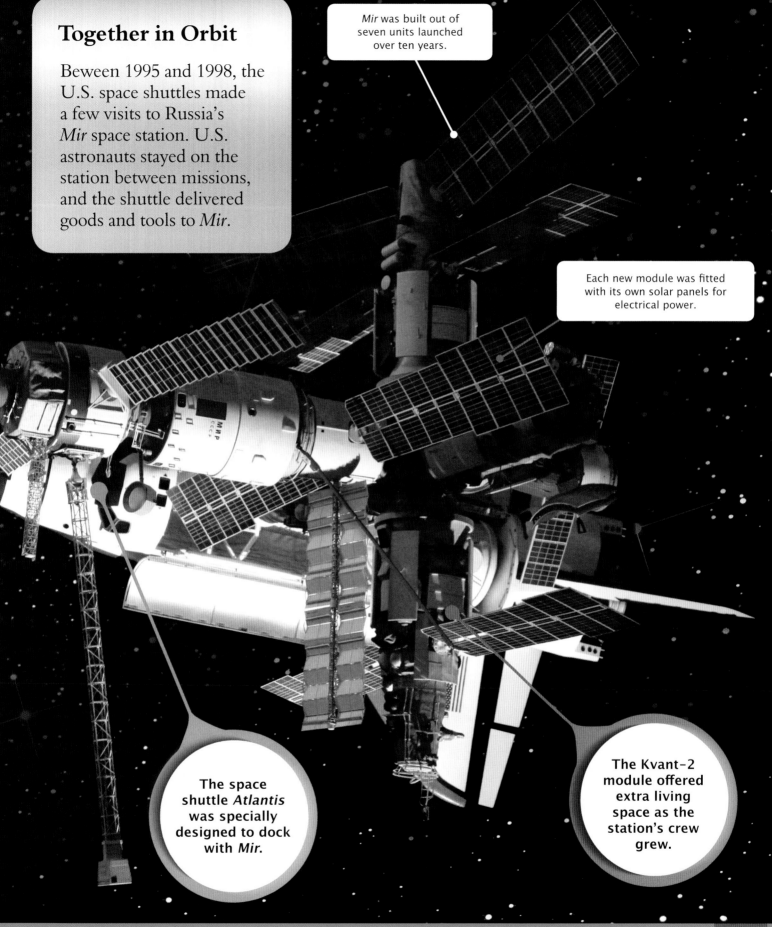

Together in Orbit

Beween 1995 and 1998, the U.S. space shuttles made a few visits to Russia's *Mir* space station. U.S. astronauts stayed on the station between missions, and the shuttle delivered goods and tools to *Mir*.

Mir was built out of seven units launched over ten years.

Each new module was fitted with its own solar panels for electrical power.

The space shuttle *Atlantis* was specially designed to dock with *Mir*.

The Kvant-2 module offered extra living space as the station's crew grew.

DID YOU KNOW? In 1997, **supply spacecraft** without crew on board crashed into *Mir*, creating damage that almost forced the crew to leave the station.

International Space Station

The ISS's solar panels can produce (make) up to 110 kW of power.

The *International Space Station* (*ISS*) is the ninth space station that humans have built in space. It is the first one where agencies from different countries have worked together—16 nations are part of the project. The *ISS* is the largest and most expensive spacecraft ever built.

Panel Power

The *ISS* has eight pairs of solar panels. Solar cells in the panels change energy from the Sun into electricity. A system of trusses (joining corridors) connects the different modules. They hold electrical lines, cooling lines for machines, and mobile transporter rails. The solar panels and robotic arms fix to the trusses, too.

Zvezda docking port

Solar panel

EACH SOLAR PANEL MEASURES MORE THAN THE WINGSPAN OF A BOEING 777.

DID YOU KNOW? Canadarm 2, the *ISS*'s main robotic arm, is 16.7 m (55 ft) long and can lift weights up to 116 tonnes (127.8 tons).

Life on the Station

The *ISS* has three laboratories: the Columbus laboratory, the Kibo laboratory and the U.S. Destiny laboratory. Every day, *ISS* crew carry out science experiments in the labs, and scientists on Earth also take part. There are research projects into making new materials and growing special crystals.

Kibo laboratory

U.S. Destiny laboratory

Columbus laboratory

Canadarm 2

NASA astronaut Karen Nyberg at work in the U.S. Destiny laboratory.

The first *ISS* module launched into orbit was the Russian–built Zarya, in 1998.

SPACECRAFT PROFILE

Name: *International Space Station*
Launch date: 1998 (latest module, 2021)
Width: 109 m (358 ft)
Length: 88 m (289 ft)
Weight: 419.6 tonnes (462.5 tons)
Orbiting speed: 8 km/s (17,895.5 mph)
Crew size: 3–6 people

Satellites

Satellites are robot spacecraft put in orbit around Earth to do a many different jobs. Some watch the weather, or photograph our planet to learn more about it. Others help us communicate, or find our way around the world.

Different Orbits

Satellites are put into an orbit that is best for the job they have to do. Some sit happily in a Low Earth Orbit (LEO) that puts them just beyond the atmosphere. Others enter much higher geostationary (fixed) orbit above the equator, where they stay above a single point on Earth's surface. Satellites that try to study the whole of Earth's surface are put in tilted orbits that loop above and below the Earth's poles as the planet rotates beneath them.

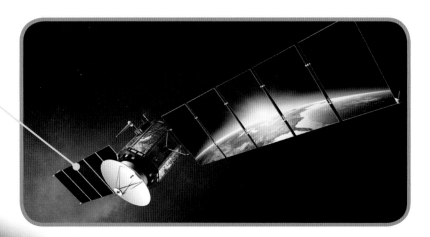

Communications satellites often use geostationary orbits.

Cameras take images of Europe and Africa every 15 minutes.

SPACECRAFT PROFILE

Name: *Meteosat 10*
Launch date: 5 July 2012
Diameter: 3.2 m (10.5 ft)
Height: 2.4 m (7.9 ft)
Orbit: 35,786 km (22,236 miles)
Orbital period: 23 h 56 m (matching Earth's rotation)

DID YOU KNOW? The **higher** a satellite orbits, the longer it takes to go around the Earth.

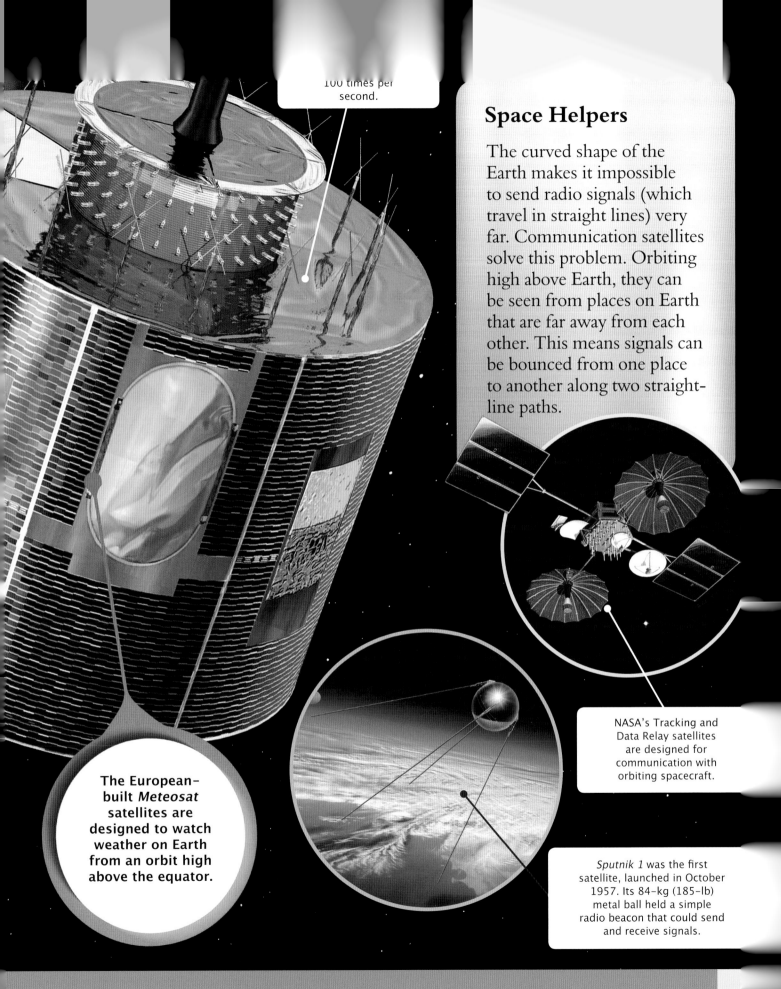

100 times per second.

Space Helpers

The curved shape of the Earth makes it impossible to send radio signals (which travel in straight lines) very far. Communication satellites solve this problem. Orbiting high above Earth, they can be seen from places on Earth that are far away from each other. This means signals can be bounced from one place to another along two straight-line paths.

The European-built *Meteosat* satellites are designed to watch weather on Earth from an orbit high above the equator.

NASA's Tracking and Data Relay satellites are designed for communication with orbiting spacecraft.

Sputnik 1 was the first satellite, launched in October 1957. Its 84-kg (185-lb) metal ball held a simple radio beacon that could send and receive signals.

Space Probes

Humans have not made it farther into space than the Moon, but we have still been able to explore much of the solar system using space probes. These robot explorers have now visited all the major planets and many smaller worlds, too.

Voyager 2 was one of a pair of spacecraft that flew past the giant planets of the outer solar system in the 1970s and 1980s.

Specialist Robots

Probes are designed to carry out one kind of mission. Some probes are orbiters that will become satellites of other planets. Others may carry out high-speed flyby missons and collect information as they fly past. Some probes are built to land on the surface of planets or moons, and even drive across their surface.

The *Huygens* lander was designed to parachute into the atmosphere of Saturn's moon, Titan.

SPACECRAFT PROFILE

Name: *Voyager 2*
Launch date: 20 August 1977
Weight: 825.5 kg (1,820 lb)
Electrical power: 470 W
Current speed: 55,000 km/h (34,000 mph)
Targets: Jupiter, Saturn, Uranus, and Neptune

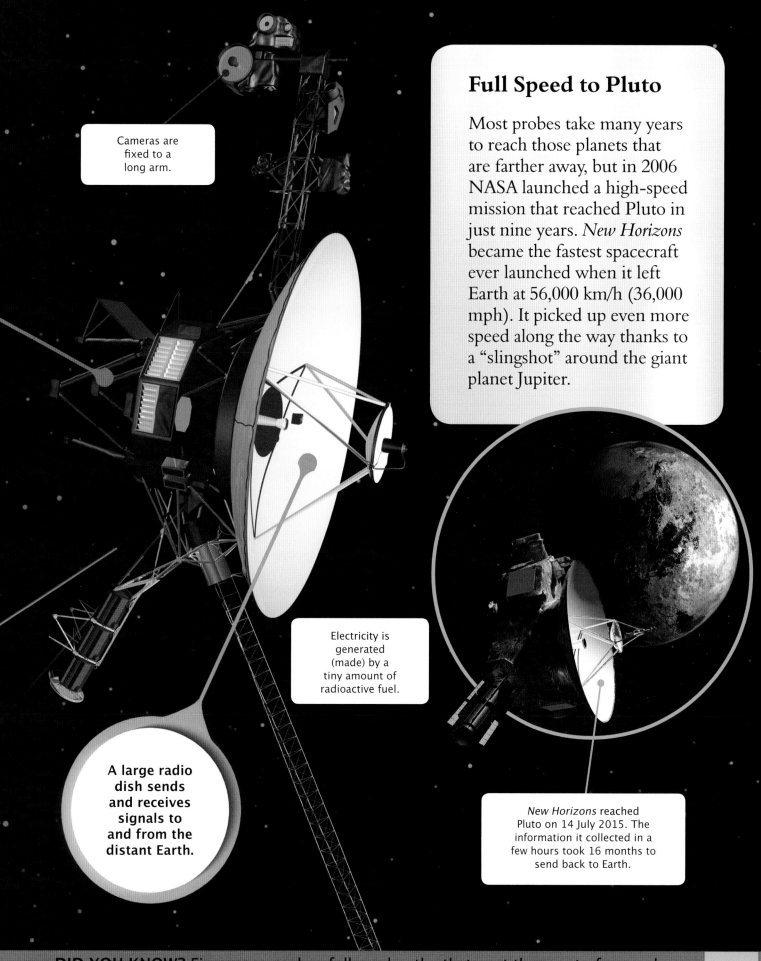

Cameras are fixed to a long arm.

Full Speed to Pluto

Most probes take many years to reach those planets that are farther away, but in 2006 NASA launched a high-speed mission that reached Pluto in just nine years. *New Horizons* became the fastest spacecraft ever launched when it left Earth at 56,000 km/h (36,000 mph). It picked up even more speed along the way thanks to a "slingshot" around the giant planet Jupiter.

Electricity is generated (made) by a tiny amount of radioactive fuel.

A large radio dish sends and receives signals to and from the distant Earth.

New Horizons reached Pluto on 14 July 2015. The information it collected in a few hours took 16 months to send back to Earth.

DID YOU KNOW? Five space probes followed paths that sent them out of our solar system altogether. Each holds a **message** from Earth for any aliens that may find it.

The Future

Although astronauts have not travelled farther than Earth's orbit since the early 1970s, space probes have flown much farther and changed our view of the solar system. In the next few years, however, we should finally begin a new age of space missions with crews on board.

Terraforming Mars

Mars has a lot more to offer than the Moon when it comes to creating new living spaces for humans on another world. The main problem is that it is a lot farther away. In the future, though, some scientists think we might be able to change the planet's climate and "terraform" it into a world much more like Earth.

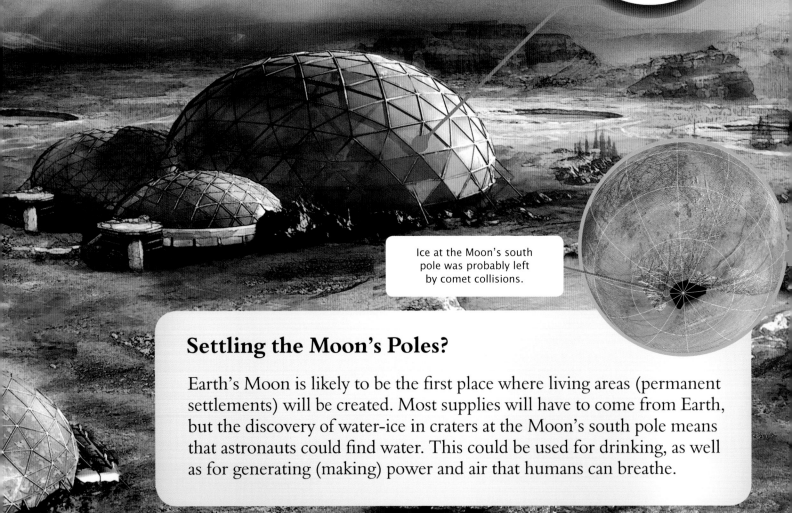

Living domes keep Earth-like air inside, protecting those inside from the thin, toxic Martian atmosphere.

Ice at the Moon's south pole was probably left by comet collisions.

Settling the Moon's Poles?

Earth's Moon is likely to be the first place where living areas (permanent settlements) will be created. Most supplies will have to come from Earth, but the discovery of water-ice in craters at the Moon's south pole means that astronauts could find water. This could be used for drinking, as well as for generating (making) power and air that humans can breathe.

SPACECRAFT PROFILE

Name: Starship
Company: SpaceX
Launch date: 2020s (planned)
Height: 122 m (400 ft)
Weight: 10.5 million kg (23.1 million lb)
Payload: 450,000 kg (990,000 lb) to Mars
with refuelling in Earth orbit

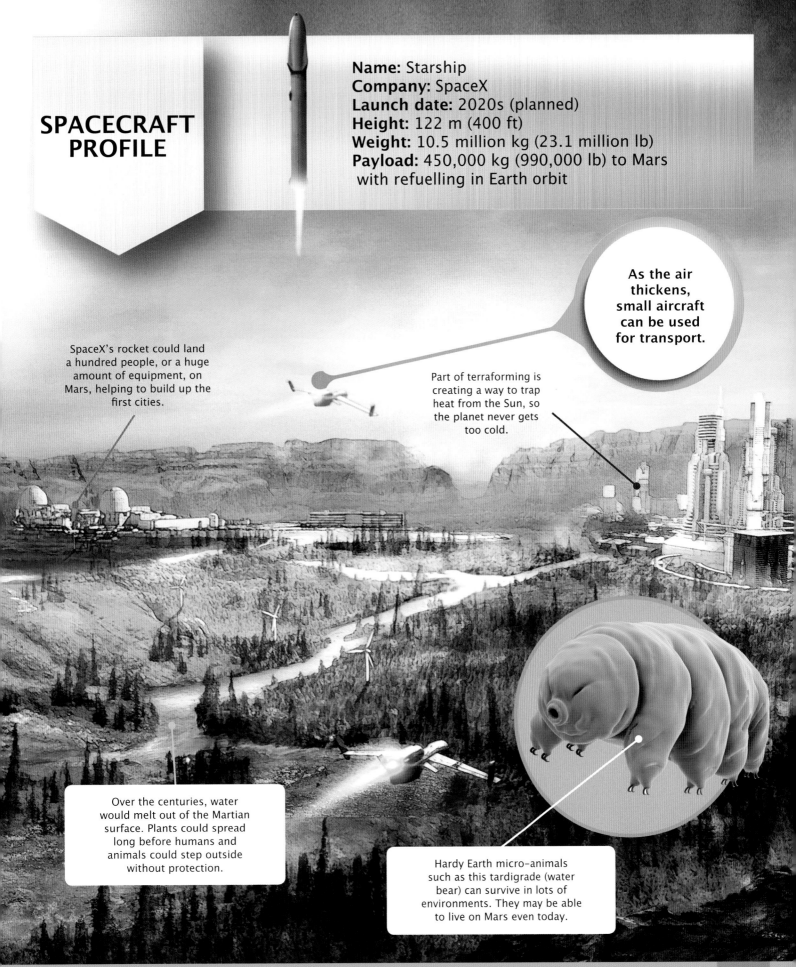

As the air thickens, small aircraft can be used for transport.

SpaceX's rocket could land a hundred people, or a huge amount of equipment, on Mars, helping to build up the first cities.

Part of terraforming is creating a way to trap heat from the Sun, so the planet never gets too cold.

Over the centuries, water would melt out of the Martian surface. Plants could spread long before humans and animals could step outside without protection.

Hardy Earth micro-animals such as this tardigrade (water bear) can survive in lots of environments. They may be able to live on Mars even today.

DID YOU KNOW? Gravity on Mars is just **40 percent** of Earth's, so the muscles of people who move to Mars may be too weak to cope back on their home planet.

The Universe

Our Universe is a massive area of space that stretches farther than we can see in every direction. It has more galaxies, stars, and planets than we could ever hope to count, and huge amounts of other material, most of which is invisible to even our most powerful telescopes.

Looking back in Time

We can only see objects in other parts of the Universe thanks to the light and other radiation we see in our telescopes. Light is the fastest thing in the Universe, so we measure huge distances in space in light-years (the distance light travels in a year, which is 9.5 trillion km or 5.9 trillion miles). The farther an object is in the Universe, the longer its light has taken to reach Earth, and the farther back in time we are seeing.

We see far-away parts of space as they were thousands or even millions of years ago, when their light set out toward us.

Curved Space

It might be hard to imagine, but space can be curved in different directions by objects with mass (weight and density). This is the basis of the force of gravity. An easier way to think about this is to imagine space as a flat rubber sheet—heavy objects create a dent within the sheet, and this will change the paths of any other objects passing nearby.

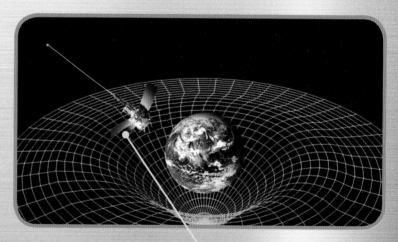

A satellite's orbit around a planet such as Earth stops it from "falling" into the curved space created by Earth's mass.

Five-sixths of matter in the Universe is dark matter, which we cannot see or measure.

Stars, gas, and dust are the main visible parts of our Universe. Other objects are hard to detect (make out).

This map shows where the 45,000 galaxies in our small part of the Universe are.

Big Bang

Our Universe was born 13.8 billion (thousand million) years ago in a huge explosion called the Big Bang. The event not only created all the matter in the Universe, but also space and time, so it is meaningless to ask where it happened, or what happened before.

Discovery

The Russian scientist Alexander Friedmann was the first person to suggest that the Universe might be expanding (growing), in 1924. The American Edwin Hubble proved this in 1929. The Belgian Georges Lemaître followed the expansion backward and stated that the Universe began in a hot, dense ball of matter.

Alexander Friedmann, the first scientist to work on the idea of an expanding Universe.

The Large Hadron Collider is a machine that recreates what the Universe was like during the Big Bang, in a much smaller space.

The Beginning

The Big Bang released huge amounts of pure energy, but as the Universe expanded, it cooled quickly and the energy was locked up within the tiniest of particles. Over the first few minutes, these particles joined together until they formed the building blocks of atoms. Atoms are the smallest particles that make up chemical elements.

The Big Bang creates all matter and energy in the Universe.

Energy changes into the tiniest of particles.

Heavy particles group together to form the cores of atoms. Small particles called electrons stay on the loose. Light waves are trapped in the fog of particles.

Electrons combine with nuclei to form first atoms. Fog clears and the Universe becomes transparent.

First stars and quasar galaxies begin to form.

13.8 BILLION YEARS AGO	+1 SECOND	+20 MINUTES	+380,000 YEARS	+150 MILLION YEARS

Galaxies and stars formed about 150 million years after the Big Bang itself.

The Universe is a huge expanding bubble, but there is no way of getting outside it.

During the Big Bang, energy could change into mass and back, creating the building blocks of matter.

DID YOU KNOW? Some astronomers think the Big Bang that started our Universe was just one of many, and that we are a tiny part of an endless "**multiverse**."

Expanding Universe

The farther away we look in space, the faster things are rushing away from us in all directions. It is a sign that the Universe as a whole is expanding, just as we would expect if it started as the explosion of the Big Bang.

Galaxies are pulled away from each other like raisins in a rising sponge cake—the farther apart they are, the faster they move away from each other.

13.8 billion years ago, the Big Bang created the Universe.

Matter formed from energy in a foggy early Universe.

The first stars and galaxies were packed quite close together.

Hubble's Law

In the mid-1920s, Edwin Hubble used a very clever way to find the distance to other galaxies. In 1929, he compared these distances to measurements of the way the galaxies moved, and found an amazing pattern—the farther away a galaxy is, the faster it is moving away from us.

Edwin Hubble discovered the expanding Universe.

DID YOU KNOW? Some astronomers think that if the Universe goes on expanding, it could tear itself apart in a **Big Rip**.

Cosmic Background

Short radio waves called microwaves, coming from every part of the Universe, are called cosmic background radiation. Discovered in 1964, they are left over from the Big Bang itself, and hold important information about the growing Universe.

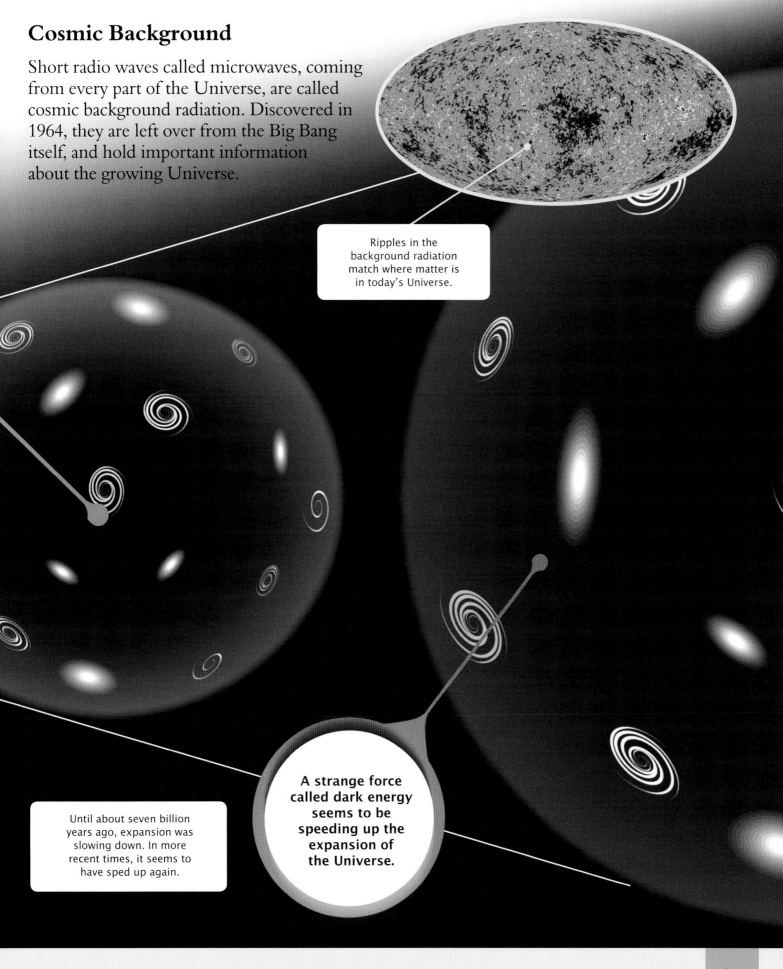

Ripples in the background radiation match where matter is in today's Universe.

A strange force called dark energy seems to be speeding up the expansion of the Universe.

Until about seven billion years ago, expansion was slowing down. In more recent times, it seems to have sped up again.

Galaxies

Galaxies are groups of stars, gas, and dust. Some are huge balls of trillions of stars and others are small clouds of just a few million. Pulled together by the force of gravity, these clouds become factories for making new stars.

Crowded Universe

Galaxies are huge objects—tens or even hundreds of thousands of light-years across, and with powerful gravity that have an effect on the galaxies nearest to them. This means that they tend to crowd together in some places, forming clusters of anything from tens to thousands of galaxies. On the largest scales, clusters join together to form superclusters that are hundreds of millions of light-years wide.

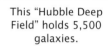

This "Hubble Deep Field" holds 5,500 galaxies.

Galaxy Types

Astronomers group galaxies into many different kinds. The most important are spirals (disks with spiral arms where the brightest stars are close together) and ellipticals (balls of red and yellow stars that look like the cores of spirals). There are also irregulars (shapeless clouds, often made up of many bright stars).

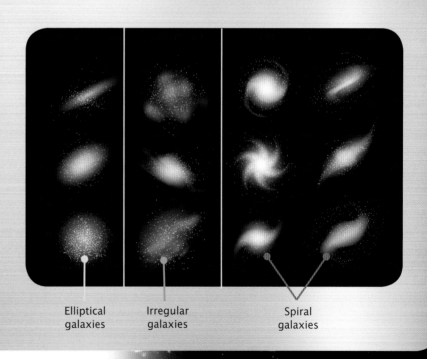

Elliptical galaxies

Irregular galaxies

Spiral galaxies

The oldest galaxies in this image look like they did 13.2 billion years ago.

This image was created when the *Hubble Space Telescope* focused on what looked like an empty area of space for 23 days.

The most distant galaxies are shapeless blobs. They are still being formed.

DID YOU KNOW? Astronomers believe there are also **dark galaxies**. These are similar to our own Milky Way, but they have hardly any stars, so they are hard to find.

How Galaxies Form

All the different types of galaxy are related to each other by how they developed. Over billions of years, galaxies join together and change type, then slowly change back—or change into something else entirely.

Galactic Chaos

Compared with objects such as stars or planets, galaxies are quite closely packed together. Collisions (crashes) happen often. When galaxies hit each other, gravity can change the orbits of stars, creating a chaotic cloud of stars that takes a long time to settle back down.

Longer-lived red and yellow stars join together in an elliptical (oval) ball.

In a spiral galaxy, bright stars form in the spiral arms.

A huge "starburst" blows away gas and stops more stars forming.

Galaxy collisions can stop stars being created.

New Stars, Old Stars

Galaxies can only form new stars if they have enough of the raw materials—gas and dust clouds. When galaxies crash again and again, the gas heats up until it is too fast-moving to form new stars. This is why old ball-shaped elliptical (oval) galaxies have very little gas and no new or young stars—they mostly have long-lived, red and yellow stars.

The Antennae Galaxies are a pair of spiral galaxies that are joining together. They are about 45 million light-years from Earth.

The central points in each galaxy will join fully in 400 million years.

A band of dust blocks light from the bright core.

Crashing gas clouds are heated and pushed together, which leads to lots of star births.

GALAXY PROFILE

Name: Antennae Galaxies
Catalogue numbers: NGC 4038 & NGC 4039
Constellation: Corvus
Distance from Earth: 45 million light-years
Description: A pair of colliding spiral galaxies with unwound spiral arms in the shape of an insect's antennae.

DID YOU KNOW? Our own Milky Way galaxy **crashing** into another (much smaller) galaxy at the moment, and will end up swallowing it completely.

Milky Way

Our home galaxy, the Milky Way, is a large spiral with a bar of stars across its middle. Our solar system orbits in the flattened disk, in the middle of two of the spiral arms and about 27,000 light-years from the star clouds that form the heart of the galaxy.

Band across the Sky

From Earth, we see the Milky Way as a band of light that wraps around the night sky. Because of its disk shape, we see more stars when we look across the disk, and many fewer when we look "up" or "down" out of the disk. The band is brightest where we look toward the middle of the galaxy.

The middle of the Milky Way lies in the constellation Sagittarius, hidden behind dense clouds of stars and dust.

Dark Secret

The orbits of stars close to the middle of the Milky Way show something surprising—they are moving very fast around a huge object with the mass of millions of Suns. Astronomers think that this object, which can't be seen directly through any telescope, is a huge black hole formed early in the Milky Way's history. Everything orbits around it.

GALAXY PROFILE

Name: Milky Way
Diameter: 120,000 light-years
Mass: Approx 1.2 trillion Suns
Number of stars: Approx 200 billion
Distance to core: 27,000 light-years
Description: Spiral galaxy with four spiral arms and a central bar of stars.

This image shows a flash of X-rays from the area around the Milky Way's central black hole. It could mark the last moments of an asteroid that moved too close and was pulled in.

The Milky Way is about 120,000 light-years across, but just 2,000 light-years thick.

Dark patches in the Milky Way are created by dust clouds that are blocking out more distant stars.

DID YOU KNOW? The word "galaxy" comes from the **Greek** for Milky Way.

97

Nearby Galaxies

The Milky Way is one of about 50 galaxies in a small, loose cluster (group) that astronomers call the Local Group. The cluster is about ten million light-years across, and is mostly made up of three large galaxies—the Milky Way, and the Andromeda and Triangulum spirals.

Ruled by Gravity

The Local Group is an area of space where the gravity of these three galaxies is slowly pulling everything together. For example, the Milky Way and Andromeda galaxies are being drawn toward an unavoidable crash that will mean they join together in about five billion years.

The Tarantula Nebula is a huge cloud of star-forming gas and dust in the Large Magellanic Cloud.

This infrared image shows the Large Magellanic Cloud as a place where a lot of stars are born.

Satellite Galaxies

The brightest galaxies of the Local Group are two irregular galaxies called the Large and Small Magellanic Clouds. Visible from Earth's southern hemisphere, they look like separate clumps of the Milky Way, but are actually in orbit around it at distances of 160,000 and 200,000 light-years. The shapes of both are changed by our galaxy's huge gravity.

GALAXY PROFILE

Name: Large Magellanic Cloud (LMC)
Constellation: Dorado and Mensa
Distance from Earth: 160,000 light-years
Size: 15,000 light-years wide
Description: A galaxy with some signs of a spiral structure, including a central bar.

DID YOU KNOW? The Tarantula Nebula's central star cluster is home to the most **massive star** so far discovered—a monster with the mass of about 310 Suns.

Strange Galaxies

Quite a lot of galaxies seem to release more radiation—both light and other types—than their stars alone are able to. Astronomers call these "active galaxies," and they think their activity comes from a monster black hole tearing matter apart.

Different Kinds of Activity

When astronomers first found active galaxies, they thought they were looking at many different objects. Some galaxies have huge clouds of radio waves around them; others seem quite normal except for a slightly brighter core. The most impressive are quasars, where the core shines so brightly that the light of the galaxy around it can't be seen.

The core of galaxy M106 appears bright because of its active nucleus.

A quasar has a brightly shining disk at its core (middle).

Centaurus A is a nearby "radio galaxy."

Heart of the Matter

The different types of galaxy are all formed because of an object called an active galactic nucleus. This is a central area where stars, gas, and dust are being pulled into a giant black hole. As they are, they form a superhot disk that releases very bright light and other radiations. Jets of particles "spat out" from above and below the disk billow out into huge clouds of radio waves.

Water heated up around the central black hole causes the galaxy to release large amounts of microwave radiation.

A view down the jet of an active galactic nucleus.

GALAXY PROFILE

Name: Messier 106
Constellation: Canes Venatici
Distance from Earth: 23.5 million light-years
Diameter: 60,000 light-years
Description: A distorted spiral "Seyfert" galaxy with an unusually bright core.

DID YOU KNOW? Collisions between galaxies often seem to "wake up" their central black holes and turn them into **active galactic cores**.

101

Dark Matter

One of the strangest things about our Universe is that everything we see and measure is just a tiny part of everything there is. The visible Universe of stars and galaxies is dwarfed by five times as much dark matter, a strange substance that doesn't release or take in radiation of any kind. This makes it totally invisible.

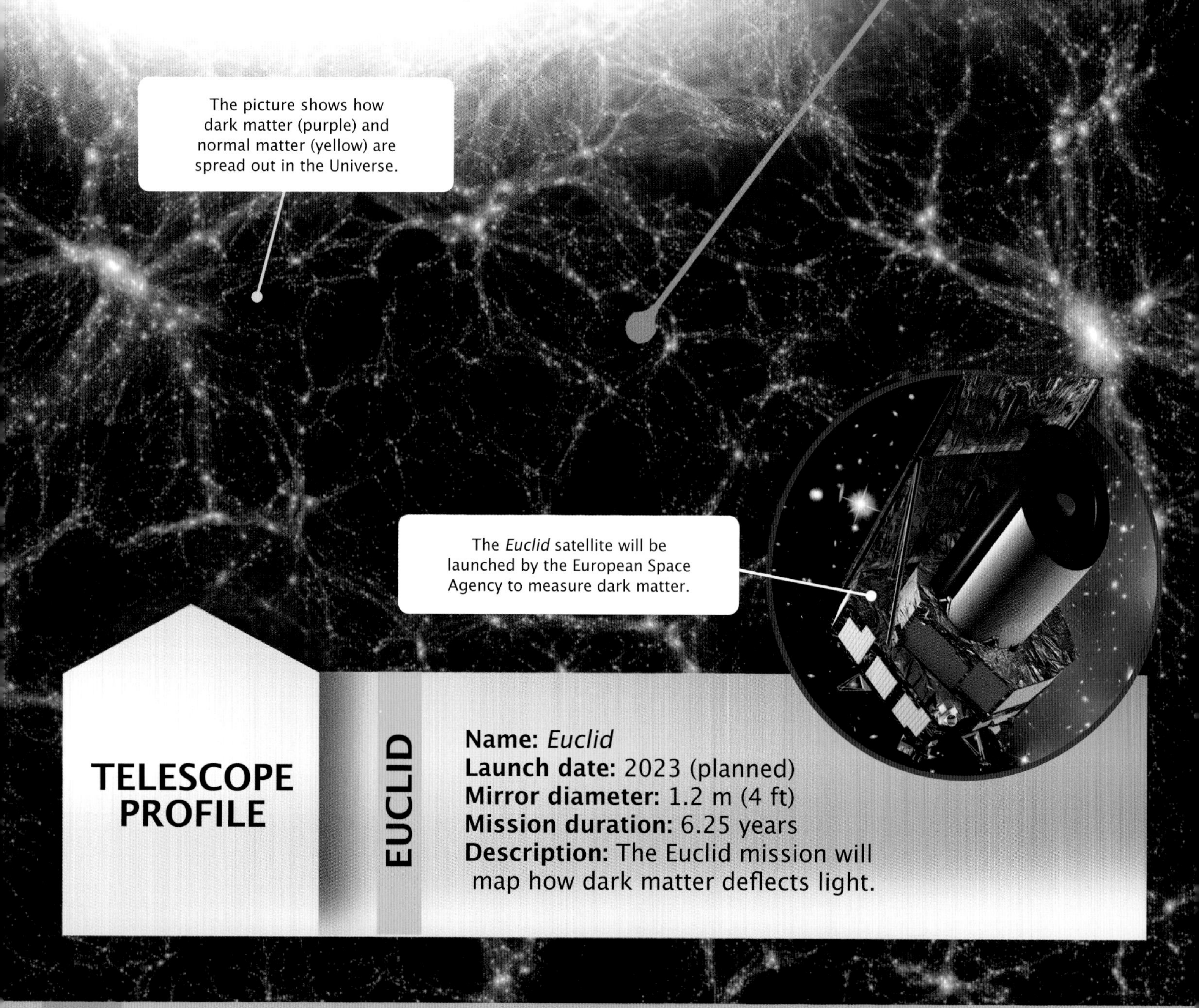

Pictures like this one, created on a computer, help scientists to work out where dark matter is compared to visible objects, such as galaxy clusters.

The picture shows how dark matter (purple) and normal matter (yellow) are spread out in the Universe.

The *Euclid* satellite will be launched by the European Space Agency to measure dark matter.

TELESCOPE PROFILE

EUCLID

Name: *Euclid*
Launch date: 2023 (planned)
Mirror diameter: 1.2 m (4 ft)
Mission duration: 6.25 years
Description: The Euclid mission will map how dark matter deflects light.

DID YOU KNOW? Astronomers call the undiscovered forms of dark matter **WIMPs**—short for "Weakly Interacting Massive Particle."

What is Dark Matter?

Astronomers used to think there were two possible explanations for dark matter. Small, dense clumps of "normal matter" such as planets and black holes might be too dark for our telescopes to discover, or there could be a completely different type of particle unknown to science. In the past few years it has become clear that unseen normal matter cannot add up to the amount of matter that must make up the Universe, so the hunt is on for strange new particles.

Telltale Traces

Dark matter can be found through gravity. It was first discovered by the way it changed the movement of stars and galaxies. Today astronomers can also find out where it is by looking at the way that it bends space and deflects (changes the path of) light from far-away galaxies.

This map shows where galaxies (yellow), hot gas (pink), and dark matter (blue) are in a galaxy cluster called the Bullet.

Gravity from large areas of dark matter in the early Universe may have decided where galaxy clusters and superclusters developed.

Alien Life

Are we alone in the Universe? It's one of the biggest questions in astronomy. New discoveries of planets around other stars and welcoming environments in our solar system mean that life could be common. But intelligent aliens are a very different matter.

Full of Life?

New discoveries have shown that some bacteria (tiny forms of life) can live in environments that we thought were uninhabitable (impossible to live in). We also now know that the basic chemicals for life are found across our galaxy. If life will automatically happen wherever the conditions are right, then there should be a lot of it in our galaxy.

Life would probably start out as simplelife forms. However, that doesn't mean that it would develop into the same forms that it has on Earth.

MOON PROFILE

Name: Europa
Moon of: Jupiter
Diameter: 3,100 km (1,900 miles)
Orbital period: 3.55 days
Description: With a deep water ocean and undersea volcanoes beneath its icy crust, there could have been life on Europa.

DID YOU KNOW? At least **six** of the solar system's moons probably have **oceans** hidden beneath their surface.

The Gray aliens described by many "alien abduction" victims are more like fairytale monsters than realistic alien life.

Our planet has few resource that any aliens who could travel here would want to take.

Alien Invaders

For many years, people have been fascinated by the idea that aliens might want to take over our planet. In reality, an invasion is very unlikely. Travel between star systems is such a huge challenge that it may simply be impossible to do. Hopefully any life forms that were able to reach that level of technology would feel no need to behave in this way toward others.

Alien invasions are the stuff of movies. Any extraterrestrial species (life forms that aren't from Earth) with the technology to travel between the stars probably wouldn't need to take over other planets.

Stars

Almost every light you see in the night sky is a star (apart from satellites or aircraft). Stars are the only objects in the Universe that truly shine, or make their own light. Everything else, from planets to glowing clouds of gas, is only reflecting or absorbing (taking in) starlight.

Star Power

A star is simply a huge ball of gas that shines by changing light chemical elements (usually hydrogen) into heavier ones (usually helium). The process is called nuclear fusion, but astronomers still talk about stars "burning" their fuel supplies.

Measuring Stars

Even powerful telescopes cannot turn most stars into anything more than pinpricks of light, but astronomers can still find out an amazing amount. The wavelengths of light that a star releases can tells us about its surface temperature and chemical make-up. The star's movement in the sky compared to other stars can show its mass, and perhaps its distance from Earth.

The *Gaia* satellite uses tiny changes in the position of stars to work out how far away they are.

TELESCOPE PROFILE

Name: *Gaia*
Launched: 2013
Mirror diameter: 1.45 x 0.5 m (4.8 x 1.6 ft)
Weight: 1,392 kg (3,069 lb)
Mission duration: Five years (planned)
Description: *Gaia* will measure the exact positions of one billion stars in the Milky Way.

The stars visible with the naked eye can be just a few light-years away or more than a thousand.

A star's brightness in the sky is called its magnitude. The brighter a star, the lower its magnitude.

Stars vary in brightness. Dwarfs are a thousand times fainter than the Sun, and giants are a million times brighter.

Sirius, the Dog Star, is the brightest star in the sky and one of the closest (8.6 light-years away). It has a faint twin star called Sirius B.

DID YOU KNOW? Sirius B is the **white dwarf** left behind by a star that was once brighter than Sirius itself.

Types of Star

The fact that stars have very different brightnesses and vary in hue from red to blue tells us that they are very different from each other. A star's brightness depends on the amount of energy it produces. Its tint tells us the temperature of its surface—red stars are cool, yellow stars hotter, and blue stars the hottest of all.

The Main Sequence

When you look at a large enough number of stars, a pattern starts to show. Cool red stars are fainter and hot blue ones are much brighter. Bright red stars are very rare, and so are faint blue ones. The link between temperature and energy output lasts for most of a star's lifetime. Astronomers call it the "main sequence" relationship.

The Witch Head Nebula is a cloud of dust and gas close to Rigel, which shines by reflecting the star's light.

STAR PROFILE

Name: Rigel
Distance: 860 light–years
Constellation: Orion
Mass: 23 Suns
Brightness: At least 120,000 Suns
Surface temperature: 12,100 °C (21,800 °F)
Star type: Blue supergiant

DID YOU KNOW? The Sun is about halfway through its ten billion years on the main sequence. After that it will swell to a **red giant** and may swallow the Earth!

Rigel is a blue supergiant star that marks the knee of the constellation Orion (the Hunter).

Life Spans of Stars

Exactly where a star sits on the "main sequence" depends on its mass, just how much fuel it has, and how fast it burns. Low-mass stars called red dwarfs burn their fuel very slowly and so can shine for tens of billions of years. Middling ones like our Sun use up their fuel in about ten billion years. Really massive stars burn fast and bright, lasting just a few million years.

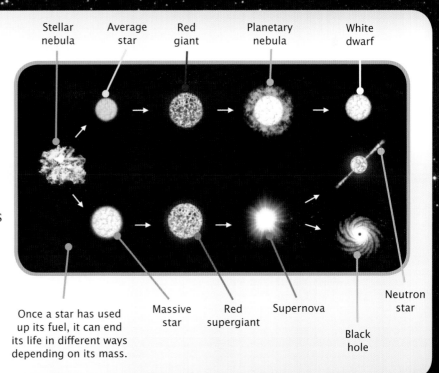

Stellar nebula

Average star

Red giant

Planetary nebula

White dwarf

Once a star has used up its fuel, it can end its life in different ways depending on its mass.

Massive star

Red supergiant

Supernova

Neutron star

Black hole

Star Birth

Stars are born in huge clouds of gas and dust called nebulae. They begin their lives as collapsing knots of gas that grow hotter and denser for perhaps a million years, until conditions at the core are able to turn hydrogen into helium.

Infrared shines through the dust to show glowing gas, warmed by newborn stars.

An infrared view of part of the Horsehead Nebula region of Orion.

Brought into Being

Star-birth nebulae are some of the most beautiful sights in the Universe. As the stars inside begin to shine, they make the gas nearby glow. Different elements create red, green, yellow, and other hues. Streams of particles blowing off the surface of the stars shape their surroundings into all kinds of shapes.

NEBULA PROFILE

Name: Horsehead Nebula
Catalogue number: Barnard 33
Distance: 1,500 light-years
Constellation: Orion
Size: Approx 3 light-years long
Description: A dark cloud of gas and dust made visible by brighter gas glowing in the background.

STAR-FORMING NEBULAE

Carina

Eagle

Horsehead

This nebula is the largest and brightest in the sky, but is only visible in southern skies.

Stars are born inside these towers of gas and dust in the constellation Serpens, the Snake.

Seen as a whole, the famous Horsehead Nebula in Orion looks like a chesspiece.

The Horsehead is just one part of a much larger star factory.

DID YOU KNOW? Much of the constellation of Orion is filled with star-forming **gas clouds**, including the famous Orion Nebula (page 124).

Star Death

When a star runs out of hydrogen to burn in its core, it is the beginning of the end. Stars have different ways to keep shining for a while longer, but they all run out of energy in the end. What happens next depends on the mass of the star.

Red Giants

As its main fuel supply runs out, a star goes through many internal (inside) changes. Its core actually gets hotter and it starts to burn hydrogen closer to the surface. This makes the star brighter, but it also makes it grow very large, so its surface is farther away from the hot core and cools. It is now a red giant.

The Cat's Eye Nebula was first observed by William Herschel in 1786.

Betelgeuse in the constellation Orion is a red supergiant star.

Explosive Death

A star with about the mass of our own Sun never makes it past the red giant stage. As it grows, it starts to vibrate (quickly grow bigger and then smaller again and again). In the end, it throws off its outer layers. High-mass stars, however, keep burning fuel and making heavier elements in their cores. When they become unstable, this leads to a sudden and violent explosion called a supernova.

Supernova explosions are rare, but can outshine an entire galaxy for a short while.

DID YOU KNOW? Planetary nebulae are short-lived compared to other objects in space—while some stars shine for billions of years, they glow for just **10,000** years.

Over millions of years, white dwarfs slowly lose their heat and turn into black dwarfs.

The Cat's Eye is a beautiful planetary nebula created as a dying, Sun-like star blows out complex bubbles of gas during its last years.

NEBULA PROFILE

Name: Cat's Eye Nebula
Catalogue number: NGC 6543
Distance: 3,300 light-years
Constellation: Draco
Size: Approx 0.5 light-years wide
Description: A planetary nebula with complex bubbles that may be shaped by an unseen twin star.

Neutron Stars

Neutron stars are all that is left behind when a supernova tears a monster star apart at the end of its life. They have the mass of a star like our own Sun, tightly packed into a sphere (ball) the size of a city.

Cosmic Lighthouses

As a star's core breaks into a neutron star, its rotation speeds up a lot. At the same time, its magnetic field grows much stronger, until it forces all of the star's radiation into two thin beams. The neutron star has become a flashing cosmic lighthouse called a pulsar.

The fastest pulsars spin hundreds of times per second.

Inside a Neutron Star

During a supernova explosion, a giant star's core is compressed (squeezed) with so much force that its atoms break down completely. Subatomic particles (smaller than an atom) called protons and electrons, with positive and negative electric charges, are then forced together to make uncharged neutrons. The neutrons stop the star from breaking apart by knocking into each other.

The searing-hot surface of a neutron star gives off most of its energy as X-rays.

DID YOU KNOW? The Crab Pulsar formed in a supernova that was recorded by stargazers around the world in **1054** CE.

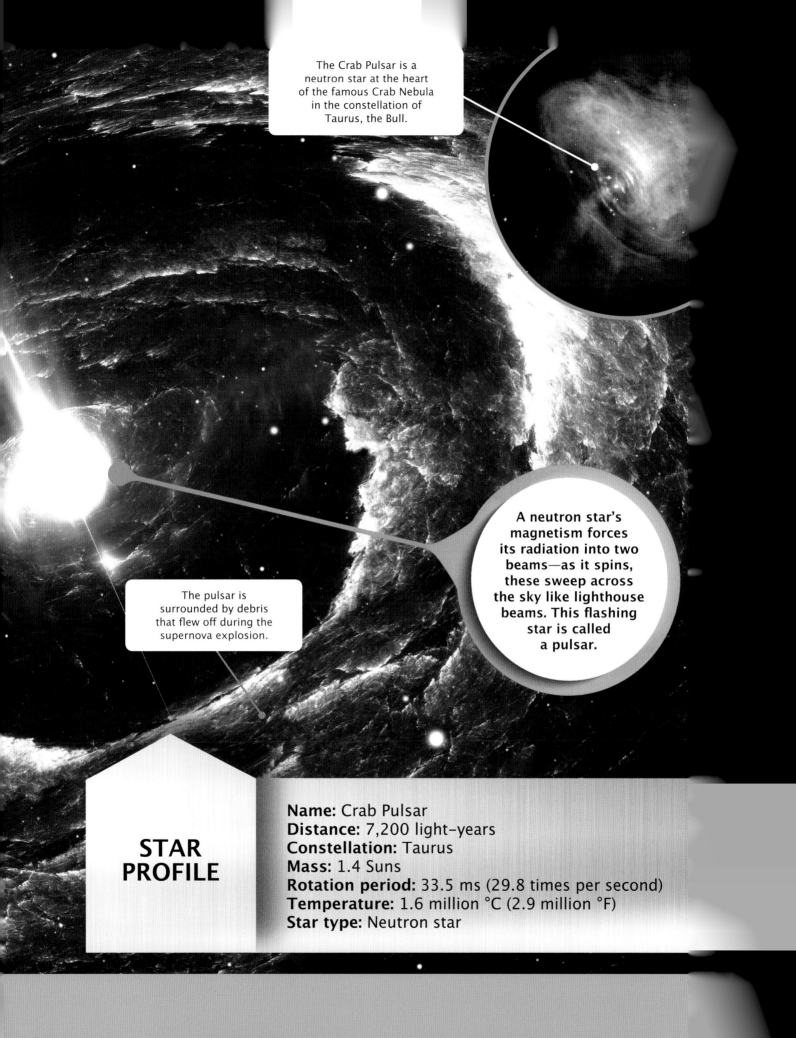

The Crab Pulsar is a neutron star at the heart of the famous Crab Nebula in the constellation of Taurus, the Bull.

The pulsar is surrounded by debris that flew off during the supernova explosion.

A neutron star's magnetism forces its radiation into two beams—as it spins, these sweep across the sky like lighthouse beams. This flashing star is called a pulsar.

STAR PROFILE

Name: Crab Pulsar
Distance: 7,200 light–years
Constellation: Taurus
Mass: 1.4 Suns
Rotation period: 33.5 ms (29.8 times per second)
Temperature: 1.6 million °C (2.9 million °F)
Star type: Neutron star

Black Holes

The strangest objects in the Universe, black holes are formed by the death of the largest stars of all. With gravity so strong that not even light can escape, they pull anything that passes too close to its doom. A blast of radiation is the only sign the object was ever there.

Birth of a Black Hole

When the core of a dying giant star breaks apart (collapses) and has more than twice the mass of the Sun, it does not stop collapsing at the neutron star stage. Instead, the neutrons themselves are torn apart and the core shrinks to a tiny size. As its gravity grows strong enough to prevent light from escaping, it forms a black hole.

A computer image shows two black holes joining together.

A black hole itself is almost invisible. However, as it feeds it creates a disk of superhot material that releases X-rays as it spirals inwards.

SPACECRAFT PROFILE

Name: *Chandra X-ray Observatory*
Launched: 1999
Mirror diameter: 1.2 m (3.9 ft)
Weight: 4,790 kg (10,560 lb)
Description: NASA's main X-ray observatory, which has discovered many new black holes.

DID YOU KNOW? According to English physicist **Stephen Hawking**, black holes slowly lose energy and disappear over billions of years.

Objects falling into a black hole are torn to pieces by gravity before being dragged into the black hole itself.

Twisted magnetic fields around black holes can create jets of particles that shoot out into space.

The Event Horizon

The black hole has a border, called its event horizon, that seals the core off from the rest of the Universe. Once it reaches the event horizon, an object has to travel faster than light to escape the black hole's pull. Inside the black hole, the core may carry on collapsing to a point in space called a singularity.

Interstellar Space

The space between the stars is far from empty—it's full of gas, dust, and particles that form the raw material for new stars. In this way, our galaxy and are like massive recyclers, remixing the same material and repackaging it into new stars.

Cosmic Recycling

Since the birth of the Universe, each new star has added more heavy elements to the light ones that formed in the Big Bang. These include elements such as oxygen and carbon, which make up our planet and play a key role in life itself. We are all made of star stuff.

The Veil Nebula is a growing bubble of debris released by a supernova explosion more than 5,000 years ago.

Cycles of Star Birth

Astronomers think that star birth is often started when shockwaves from earlier supernova explosions meet clouds of star-forming material. Growing supernova debris also adds heavy elements to the star-forming nebula. Some elements end up in the new stars, and others that form planets.

Heavy elements form the dark dust in star-forming particles.

NEBULA PROFILE

Name: Western Veil Nebula
Catalogue number: NGC 6960
Distance: 1,470 light-years
Constellation: Cygnus
Size: Approx 90 light-years wide
Description: The remains of a supernova that covers 36 times the area of a Full Moon.

Gas in the expanding (growing) nebula is heated to temperatures of 150,000 °C (270,000 °F).

The remains of the supernova are made up of elements including hydrogen, oxygen, and carbon. These will one day find their way into new stars.

DID YOU KNOW? Stars that have a large amounts of **heavy elements** from interstellar space shine more brightly, but have shorter lifespans.

Star Groups

Because stars are born together in "nurseries" of star-forming nebulae, they are usually found in loose groups called open clusters. Over tens of millions of years, these star clouds slowly drift apart, but some stars stick together all their lives.

Binaries and Multiples

Sometimes, the slowly spinning clumps of gas that form stars split into two or more regions. Each of these can then give birth to a star, leading to a pair or group of stars locked in orbit around each other. This is called a binary or multiple system. Because their stars were born at the same time, these systems can tell us a lot about the life cycles of stars.

Starlight reflects off nearby dust to surround the Pleiades with a blue glow.

Albireo in the constellation Cygnus, the Swan, is a beautiful binary pair of blue and orange stars.

CLUSTER PROFILE

Name: Pleiades or Seven Sisters
Catalogue number: Messier 45
Distance: 450 light–years
Constellation: Taurus
Size: Approx 30 light–years wide
Description: A cluster of at least 1,000 stars that formed together about 100 million years ago.

DID YOU KNOW? Five of the brightest stars in the famous constellation of **Ursa Major** (the Great Bear) began life in the same open cluster.

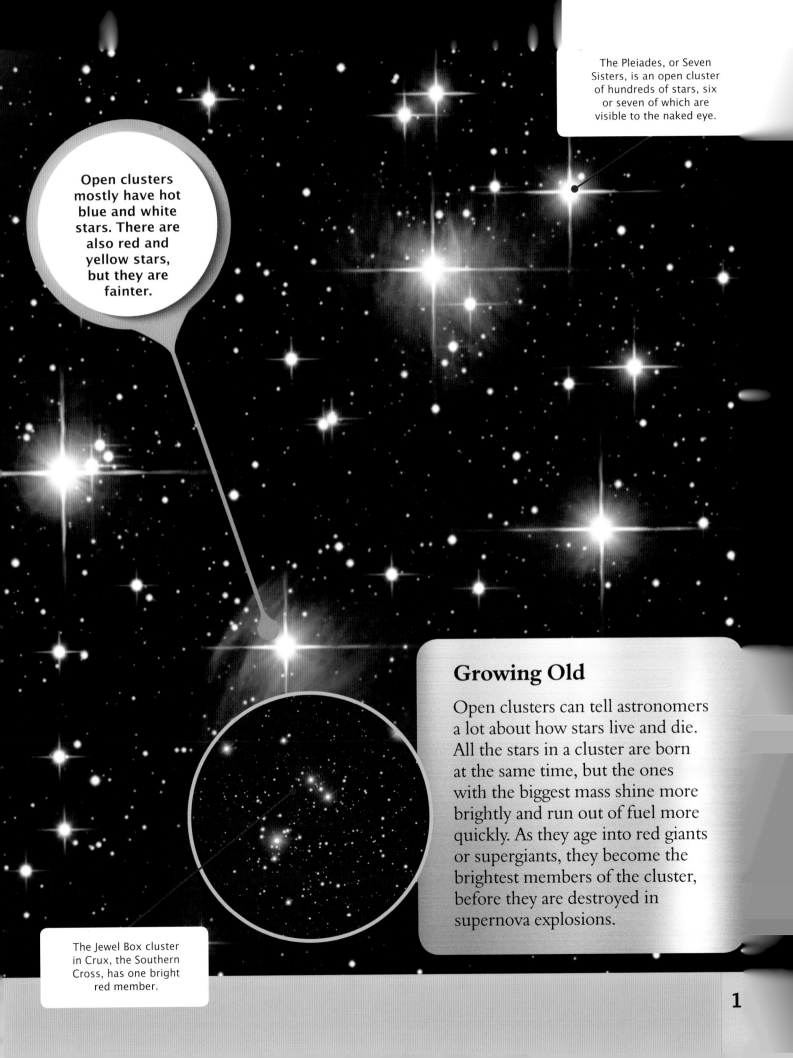

The Pleiades, or Seven Sisters, is an open cluster of hundreds of stars, six or seven of which are visible to the naked eye.

Open clusters mostly have hot blue and white stars. There are also red and yellow stars, but they are fainter.

Growing Old

Open clusters can tell astronomers a lot about how stars live and die. All the stars in a cluster are born at the same time, but the ones with the biggest mass shine more brightly and run out of fuel more quickly. As they age into red giants or supergiants, they become the brightest members of the cluster, before they are destroyed in supernova explosions.

The Jewel Box cluster in Crux, the Southern Cross, has one bright red member.

Globular Clusters

Very different from open star clusters, globular clusters are tight, compact balls with tens or hundreds of thousands of stars closely packed together. The stars in globular clusters are ancient compared to most of the ones we see in other parts of the galaxy.

Some astronomers think that Omega Centauri might be the core of a galaxy torn apart by the Milky Way.

Distant Blobs

Globular clusters are much more difficult to see in the sky than open clusters and are many thousands of light-years away from Earth. They are only found around the middle of our galaxy and above and below its disk in a region called the halo. Their small size (usually a few tens of light-years across), means they look like fuzzy blobs.

Messier 13 in the constellation of Hercules is the brightest globular cluster in the northern sky.

Globular Beginnings

The old stars in globular clusters are red and yellow, and less massive than the Sun. There are no young hot stars, and no star-forming gas. Astronomers think that globulars formed during ancient galaxy collisions that created huge star clusters. While heavier stars in these clusters aged and died, the longer-lived, red and yellow stars survived until today.

CLUSTER PROFILE

Name: Omega Centauri
Catalogue number: NGC 5139
Distance: 15,800 light-years
Constellation: Centaurus
Size: Approx 150 light-years wide
Description: The largest and densest of the Milky Way's globular clusters, with about ten million stars.

DID YOU KNOW? The Milky Way galaxy has more than 150 globular clusters orbiting it, but the distant egg-shaped galaxy **M87** has more than 12,000!

123

Exoplanets

Over the past few years, astronomers have discovered more than a thousand exoplanets—planets orbiting stars outside our solar system. They have also found signs of many more being born, but these worlds are often very different from Earth.

Planets form in nebulae that are rich in dust made from heavier elements, such as that in the Orion Nebula.

How Planets are Born

As stars leave their birth nebulae, they are often surrounded by a flattened disk called a proplyd. Over time, the material in this disk starts to clump together until some clumps have enough gravity to pull in more gas and dust from their surroundings. Once this has happened, they quickly grow into protoplanets, which crash and form planets.

The *Hubble Space Telescope* discovered that many newborn stars in the Orion Nebula are surrounded by proplyds.

DID YOU KNOW? The closest star to Earth, a faint **red dwarf** called Proxima Centauri, is orbited by an Earth-like planet that could have water on its surface.

Planet Hunting

Astronomers use two main methods to look for planets. One way is to look for the tiny wobbles in a star's movement that are caused by an orbiting planet pulling it in different directions. Another is to watch for tiny dips in a star's brightness that happen when a planet is passing in front of it. With both methods it is easier to find giant planets, similar to Jupiter, rather than smaller ones.

Planet hunters have found a lot of "hot Jupiters"—giant exoplanets orbiting very near their stars.

This image of a planetary system called HR8799 was taken by the Keck Observatory.

NEBULA PROFILE

Name: Orion Nebula
Catalogue number: Messier 42
Distance: 1,340 light-years
Constellation: Orion
Size: Approx 25 light-years wide
Description: The heart of a huge star-forming region that spreads across Orion.

Glossary

ACTIVE GALAXY
A galaxy with a giant black hole producing extra light in its core.

ASTEROID
A small rocky object made up of material left over from the birth of the solar system.

ASTRONOMICAL UNIT
Earth's distance from the Sun—about 150 million km (93 million miles).

ATMOSPHERE
A shell of gases kept around a planet, star, or other object by its gravity.

BINARY STAR
One of a pair of stars orbiting each other.

BLACK HOLE
A superdense point in space, usually formed by a collapsed core of a giant star. A black hole's gravity is so powerful that even light cannot escape from it.

COMET
A chunk of rock and ice from the edge of the solar system. Close to the Sun, its melting ices form a coma and a tail.

CONSTELLATION
A star pattern in the sky and the area around it.

DARK MATTER
A strange, invisible substance that forms most of the mass in the Universe.

ELECTROMAGNETIC RADIATION
A type of energy that travels at the speed of light. Radiations are given different names depending on the amount of energy they carry, from low-energy radio waves, through infrared, visible light, ultraviolet, and X-rays, to the highest-energy gamma rays.

ELLIPTICAL GALAXY
An egg-shaped galaxy made up of old red and yellow stars.

EXOPLANET
A planet orbiting a star outside our solar system.

GALAXY
A large system of stars, gas, and dust with anything from millions to trillions of stars.

GIANT PLANET
A planet much larger than Earth, made up of gas, liquid, and slushy frozen chemicals.

GLOBULAR CLUSTER
A dense ball of ancient, long-lived stars, found in orbit around galaxies, such as the Milky Way.

GRAVITY
A natural force created around objects with mass, which draws other objects toward them.

IRREGULAR GALAXY
A galaxy with no clear shape, usually rich in gas, dust, and star-forming regions.

KUIPER BELT
A ring of small icy worlds directly beyond the orbit of Neptune. Pluto is the largest known Kuiper Belt Object.

LIGHT-YEAR
The distance light travels in a year—about 9.5 trillion km (5.9 trillion miles).

LUNAR ECLIPSE
When the Full Moon passes into Earth's shadow so direct sunlight does not reach its surface.

MAIN SEQUENCE
The longest phase in a star's life, when it shines by turning its main fuel source of hydrogen into helium at its core. During this time, the star's brightness and temperature are related—the brighter the star is, the hotter its surface and the bluer it looks.

MILKY WAY
Our home galaxy, a spiral with a bar across its core. Our solar system is about 28,000 light-years from the monster black hole at its heart.

MOON
Earth's closest companion in space, a ball of rock that orbits Earth every 27.3 days. Most other planets in the solar system have moons of their own.

MULTIPLE STARS
A system of two or more stars in orbit around one another.

NEBULA
A cloud of gas or dust floating in space. Nebulae are the raw material used to make stars.

NEUTRON STAR
The core of a supermassive star, left behind by a supernova explosion and collapsed to the size of a city. Many neutron stars are also pulsars.

OORT CLOUD
A spherical (ball-shaped) shell of sleeping comets, surrounding all of the solar system out to a distance of about two light-years.

OPEN CLUSTER
A large group of bright young stars that were been born in the same nebula.

ORBIT
A fixed path taken by one object in space around another because of the effect of gravity.

PLANET
A world that orbits the Sun, which has enough mass and gravity to pull itself into a ball-like shape, and clear space around it of other large objects.

PLANETARY NEBULA
A growing cloud of glowing gas thrown off from the outer layers of a dying red giant star.

POLE STAR
A star that lies close to Earth's north or south pole, and so stays more or less fixed in the sky as Earth rotates.

PULSAR
A fast-spinning neutron star whose intense magnetic field forces its radiation into two narrow beams that sweep around the sky like a lighthouse. From Earth, a pulsar appears as a quickly flashing star.

QUASAR
A distant active galaxy with a very bright core.

RED DWARF
A small, faint star with a cool red surface and less than half the mass of the Sun.

RED GIANT
A huge, brilliant (very bright)star near the end of its life, with a cool, red surface. Red giants are stars that have used up the fuel supply in their core and are going through big changes in order to keep shining for a little longer.

ROCKET
A vehicle that drives itself forward through a controlled chemical explosion and can therefore travel in the vacuum of space. Rockets are the only practical way to launch spacecraft and satellites.

ROCKY PLANET
An Earth-sized or smaller planet, made up mostly of rocks and minerals, sometimes with a thin outer layer of gas and water.

SATELLITE
Any object orbiting a planet. Moons are natural satellites made of rock and ice. Artificial (man-made) satellites are machines in orbit around Earth.

SOLAR ECLIPSE
When the Moon passes directly in front of the Sun, casting its shadow onto Earth.

SPACE PROBE
A robot vehicle that explores the solar system and sends back signals to Earth.

SPACECRAFT
A vehicle that travels into space.

SPECTRUM
The spread-out band of light with different hues, created by passing light through a prism or similar device.

SPIRAL GALAXY
A galaxy with a hub of old yellow stars (sometimes crossed by a bar) surrounded by a flattened disk of younger stars, gas, and dust. Bright newborn stars make a spiral pattern across the disk.

SUPERNOVA
An enormous explosion marking the death of a star much more massive than the Sun.

SUPERNOVA REMNANT
An expanding (growing) cloud of shredded, superhot gas left behind a supernova explosion.

TELESCOPE
A device that collects light or other radiations from space and uses them to create a bright, clear image. Telescopes can use either a lens or a mirror to collect light.

WHITE DWARF
The dense, burnt-out core of a star like the Sun, collapsed to the size of the Earth but still intensely hot.

ZODIAC
Twelve constellations surrounding the Sun's yearly path around Earth's sky. The planets and Moon are usually found within these constellations.

Index